The Word is Very Near You
Feasts and Festivals

Also by the same author and available from Canterbury Press

The Word is Very Near You: Sundays

'Pure Gold. An invaluable resource for preachers and all who wish to relate the Bible to life today.' *Canon John Young*

'Lively, imaginative, insightful and profound, these reflections penetrate to the heart of the readings and often open unexpected connections with the world's needs and longings.' *Liz Carmichael, Chaplain, St John's College, Oxford*

The Inner-City of God: The Diary of an East End Parson

'This book made me laugh out loud, but it also made me cry. It is about what it means to be faithful to Christ, even if you are not successful, which is how life is for most of us.' *Nick Holtam, Vicar of St Martin-in-the-Fields*

'John Pridmore is an Anglican hero – and one of the few writers I know capable of making me a better person.' *Giles Fraser, Canon Chancellor of St Paul's Cathedral*

'This book is and will remain unrivalled for those who wish to understand what the job of an Anglican parish priest is like.' *CR Quarterly*

www.canterburypress.co.uk

The Word is Very Near You

Feasts and Festivals

Reflections on the lectionary readings

John Pridmore

First published in 2010 by the Canterbury Press Norwich
Editorial office
13–17 Long Lane,
London, EC1A 9PN, UK

Canterbury Press is an imprint of Hymns Ancient and Modern Ltd
(a registered charity)
13A Hellesdon Park Road,
Norwich NR6 5DR, UK

www.scm-canterburypress.co.uk

British Library Cataloguing in Publication data

A catalogue record for this book is available
from the British Library

978 1 84825 031 4

Originated by The Manila Typesetting Company
Printed and bound in Great Britain by
CPI Antony Rowe, Chippenham, Wiltshire

Contents

For all the saints,
but especially for Dick

Introduction

Christians keep Sunday special – at least they are supposed to. Every Sunday is the day of resurrection, not just Easter Day. But there are weekdays too during the year that are important to Christians. Ash Wednesday and Good Friday are obvious examples. Then there are the festivals, such as Christmas Day, which only occasionally fall on a Sunday. So it is with the saints' days. St George's Day, 23 April, for example, will some years be a Sunday, but most years not. It is good for us to keep the saints' days special, on whatever day of the week they fall. We are not alone. We belong to the extended family of all the saints, those with us still but those too who rejoice 'on another shore and in a greater light'. We are surrounded by this 'great cloud of witnesses' (Hebrews 12.1) and we are glad to give thanks for them on any day of the week.

The Church of England's 'Principal Service Lectionary' provides readings both for Sundays and also for the festivals which do not – or do not necessarily – fall on a Sunday. In the first volume of *The Word is Very Near You* (Canterbury Press, 2009) I commented on the lectionary's three-year cycle of readings for the Sundays of the church year. This slimmer second volume focuses on the church's high days and holy days that are never on a Sunday or only sometimes on a Sunday. My aim is to explore the themes of these days in the light of the scriptural readings appointed for them.

King Lear, contemplating what he supposed would be indefinite imprisonment with his daughter Cordelia, imagines that they will wile away their time behind bars gossiping about 'who's in, who's out' at court. The same 'who's in, who's out' question faced me in having to decide which festivals to include in these pages. Choices had to be made. As an Englishman, I have not presumed to comment on 'the saints for Ireland, Scotland, and Wales', although the Church of England lectionary provides readings for their festivals. Because I based these studies on the provisions of the 'Principal Service Lectionary', I had to forego commenting on the men and women of God to whom are grudgingly allotted 'Lesser Festivals' or mere 'Commemorations'. Many of these brave and holy people probably mean more to us than those honoured by their red-letter days and a strong case could be made for their promotion to a higher place in the church's esteem and a more prominent place in its calendar. But that case cannot be made here.

In the end I resolved the 'who's in, who's out' issue by a simple rule of thumb. The days I mull over are those that are generally observed as 'principal festivals' in the Church of England. Rules of thumb, of course, are always rough and ready. It might be felt that there are special days not mentioned here that have as great a claim to be included as those that are discussed. Be that as it may, I am fairly confident that none of the festivals I do consider could lightly have been dropped.

Three explanatory notes are perhaps necessary. First, the lectionary provides three 'Sets' of readings which may be used 'on the evening of Christmas Eve and on Christmas Day', but it stipulates that 'Set III should be used at some service during the celebration'. The passage appointed as the Gospel in the Set III readings is the Prologue to John's Gospel (John 1.1–14). It is this text above all which compels our attention at Christmas, the attention not least of those who have the unnerving task of expounding it. For this reason, I have based all three Christmas expositions on the Set III readings.

Second, I have taken the opportunity provided by this second series of reflections to include some thoughts on four festivals which are – necessarily or probably – celebrated on Sundays, but which were not included in the previous volume. These are a Dedication Festival, Bible Sunday, Mothering Sunday and Harvest Thanksgiving.

Third, for the celebration of a Dedication Festival the lectionary provides different readings for years A, B and C. The focus of this festival will usually be on the story of the local church whose dedication is being celebrated. For this reason, I have included just one reflection for this festival, a more general consideration of the role of holy places in the mission of the church.

Many of these pieces were originally published in the *Church Times*. As I said in the foreword to this book's predecessor, I am grateful to the deputy editor of the *Church Times*, Rachel Boulding, for making my comments on the lectionary fit to appear in its pages. My deep gratitude is also due to Christine Smith of Canterbury Press, both for inviting me to prepare these studies for publication in book form and for her patience with my endless tiresome questions.

Again as I acknowledged in the foreword to the earlier book, I owe more than I can say to the encouragement and forbearance of my wife Pat, as I have tried to put into words what often is beyond words.

This book is dedicated to someone who brings to his study of Holy Scripture an immeasurably clearer and more Christian mind than mine. The book would have been much better if he had written it.

John Pridmore

FEASTS AND HOLY DAYS

Christmas Day

25 DECEMBER

Isaiah 52.7–10; Hebrews 1.1–4 (5–12); John 1.1–14

1. THE WORD OF NO FIXED ABODE

'The Word became flesh and dwelt among us.' We should translate the text literally, though few modern versions have the nerve to do so. 'The Word became flesh and *pitched his tent* among us.' The verb John uses sends us back to Old Testament stories of the God who chose to share the itinerant life of his nomadic people. 'The cloud covered the tent of meeting, and the glory of the LORD filled the tabernacle' (Exodus 40.34). The reality of camping is rarely as blissful as it seems in prospect or retrospect – I think of a certain sodden field above Morecambe – and the wilderness wanderings of the children of Israel were far from idyllic. Nevertheless those years came to be seen by the people of Israel as the honeymoon period of their relationship with God. That's how it should be between God and his people, sharing a journey, together under canvas and under the stars. Stephen saw that and said so – 'The Most High does not dwell in houses made with human hands' – and he was stoned for his pains (Acts 7.48). So there can be no more glorious a promise than Hosea's, 'I will make you live in tents again' (Hosea 12.9).

'The Word became flesh and *pitched his tent* among us.' John's language invites us to have second thoughts about the familiar Christmas stories. Joseph and Mary 'great with child' have to make the arduous journey from Nazareth to Bethlehem. There they must bed down as best they can in the byre, where soon Mary's child is born. There they are visited by shepherds, whiffy outsiders who are probably no better housed than their sheep. Astrologers from the back of beyond turn up, led on their long safari by a wandering star. While the child is still a toddler they are on the move again, this time to Egypt. As the Victorian matron remarked, 'How very different from the home life of our dear Queen!'

We speak at Christmas of all that seems bizarre about the birth of Jesus. But if we read these stories again in the light of John's interpretation of what took place when Christ was born, we find that they say something rather different. The strange circumstances of this child's birth do not set him apart from those of us who were not born in a cattle trough. On the contrary, they identify him with us. It is precisely our condition that this child is born to share. I am essentially a nomad, even if I have lived for seventy years in the same semi-detached house in Sidcup. Human beings were wandering the earth for tens of thousands of years before they settled in caves and in penthouses costing millions. The security of the roof over our heads is wholly illusory. If God had wanted us to stay in the same place he would have given us roots, not legs.

On Christmas Day we read the first few verses of the letter to the Hebrews. Were there time, we should read the eleventh chapter as well. For the anonymous writer, Christians are those who recognize that they are 'strangers and foreigners on earth', that they are Bedouin with no need of buildings. So it was for Abraham who 'set out not knowing where he was going'. So it was for all those who looked for Christ's day but who did not live to see it. So it is for us who, surrounded by these witnesses, try to follow their example. Whatever our address, we are a people with no permanent home. That 'homelessness', so far from depriving us of our humanity, constitutes it. We may be on the road for a long time yet, so we must 'lay aside every weight' (Hebrews 12.1) – surely a text for the day in the year when we put so much more weight on.

When we read that 'the Son of Man has nowhere to lay his head' (Luke 9.58) we may feel sorry for him. If so, we miss the point. (As does the weepy carol, 'Thou didst leave thy throne and thy kingly crown when thou camest to earth for me.') The famous text is not there to arouse our pity. Beneath Luke's haunting words is the same Christmas truth taught by John, that the boy born in a byre shares the essential vulnerability and insecurity of our human condition, however swanky are the houses we like to think are ours. In two miraculous lines Henry Vaughan goes to the heart of the Christmas story:

He travels to be born, and then
Is born to travel more again.
('The Nativity')

An unnecessary footnote. To recognize that, wherever we live, we have 'no fixed abode' is no reason for refusing shelter to the homeless. Nor is it a reason to ignore the plight of those, massed in their thousands in our planet's countless refugee camps, whose 'tents' are plastic sheets on sticks.

2. THE STRANGLED TOWN OF BETHLEHEM

What we make of the Bible depends on where we read or hear it. Take the words with which the Prologue of St John's Gospel comes to its tremendous climax – 'The Word became flesh and dwelt among us' (John 1.14). Supposing we hear these words in an English parish church, as the Gospel at Midnight Mass or as the final reading at a service of lessons and carols. The words may well move us deeply yet still say very little. It is not that they are too familiar. It is that they don't connect. The great text hangs in the air, echoing high in the nave like the last notes of one of the carols we've been singing, but without engaging with the world beyond the church walls. But supposing this Christmas – *this* Christmas – we go to Bethlehem, to that 'strangled' little town as it has been called. Supposing we hear those climactic words in a town now encircled by walls and fences which threaten its very survival as a community. If we stop off in Bethlehem to hear John's account of the conditions under which our gentle Lord consented to be born, we'll make the necessary connection. (Online assistance is available for such imaginative journeys. Visit www.openbethlehem.org.)

Bethlehem is suffering what Christ suffered. Charles Wesley – his words more often cited than sung these days – talks of 'Our God contracted to a span'. For George Herbert, the true light coming into the world was 'glorious yet contracted light' ('Christmas'). It's all about confinement and contractions. The resonances of such imagery when we're celebrating the birth of a baby are inescapable. But for the poets, as for John, the emphasis is on the constraints of the incarnation in all its aspects. The Word made flesh is the poet Crashaw's 'Eternity shut in a span' ('In the Holy Nativity of Our Lord').

Bethlehem too is 'shut in a span'. Its imprisonment is iniquitous, but grimly apposite to the events over which our writer broods. The Word becomes flesh. Becoming flesh, he becomes all flesh is heir to. Pious tourists used to tut-tut about the tat marketed in Bethlehem's Manger Square. They objected to the commercialization of a holy place. But that's flesh for you. And in the likeness of such 'sinful flesh' (Romans 8.3) love came down.

Now the tourists and the tat are almost gone and we redirect our anger. We protest rightly that Bethlehem is being throttled, that the life of a once thriving community is being slowly extinguished. But that too – what stranglers inflict and the strangled suffer – is flesh, the flesh our Lord makes his own. Bethlehem struggles to breathe. It was asphyxia, the commentators tell us, that killed Jesus. The beleaguered little town proves a fitting birthplace for the one who bears the worst about us.

The last time I went there was by local bus. We were turned off the bus at gun-point and lined along the side while they checked our papers. That's flesh too. The space where the Word 'pitches his tent', his 'pad' as one theologian has recently called it, is a pitifully narrow enclosure. Such are the conditions – those they know about in Bethlehem – which Christ endures. Yet, according to John, it is these most unpropitious conditions which allow his glory to be seen. John delights in such contradictions. The contrasting strands are woven through his Gospel – light and darkness, life and death, truth and falsehood.

Glory suffuses this Gospel. Here a baby's flesh is bathed in it. But for John that glory will be at its most radiant when, so the other Gospels say, the sky turned black.

'The Word became flesh and dwelt among us.' What we make of the text depends on where we are. For too many of us where we are is in front of a computer screen. 'The Word' for us is 'Word for Windows'. Not the word of wisdom, not the word which addresses us personally and establishes a relationship. Not the word incarnated but the word digitized. An imaginative leap greater than that which takes us to Bethlehem is needed to return to a time when the supreme purpose of words was to let us talk to each other face to face.

The Prologue to John's Gospel harks back to the account of creation at the start of the Bible. That story too begins with a spoken word. The repeated 'God said . . .' is a command. God said – and it was done. But it is above all a bidding inviting a response. The invitation is to conversation and companionship. 'Let's be friends.' That is what words are for and that is what the Word is for. The Word become flesh embodies the invitation made to Adam, to walk and talk with God.

3. THE BORN OUTSIDER

Jesus is born outside, just as he dies outside. The door of the inn closes on the one about to be born, just as the gates of the city close on the one about to die. The opposition of 'inside' and 'outside' is present throughout the Gospel story. Jesus is never found 'inside', where it's safe and comfortable. He is neither Pharisee nor Sadducee, neither Essene nor Zealot. There is no party to protect him or to promote his cause. Those who go to him must 'go out' to him, forfeiting the security which ordinary human associations – including families – provide. Some households briefly shelter him. Perhaps they try to hold him 'inside', to curb his compulsion always to be on his way somewhere else.

But the one who, as on this day, 'pitched his tent' among us (John 1.14) can never make anywhere his permanent home. The Son of Man, with nowhere to lay his head, is always 'outside'.

This polarity of outside and inside is starkest in the accounts of his passion, where 'Christ outside' stands over against the scheming inner-circles around Caiaphas, Pilate and Herod. Finally he perishes 'outside the camp', in that waste land where, abandoning all transitory securities, we are summoned to follow him (Hebrews 13.12–13).

This tension between 'inside' and 'outside' is acute in the story of the birth of Jesus. He is born outside, with the despised and rejected; outside, where all must go who are not wanted. The ones inside Luke's inhospitable inn, those described by John as Christ's 'own' (John 1.11), do not receive him. No doubt it's warm inside, but Mary and Joseph are left out in the cold. Christians, at least in the West, have always taken it that Christ was born in winter. In fact we have no idea at what time of the year he was born. But that he was born 'in the bleak mid-winter' is a truth about the nature of Christ's coming, whatever the date of the first Christmas. It was cold outside, whatever the temperature. R. S. Thomas comments, 'The very word Christ has that thin crisp sound so suggestive of frost and snow and the small sheets of ice that crack and splinter under our feet, even as the host is broken in the priest's fingers' (*Selected Prose*, Welsh Poetry Press, 1983). In a late poem, Thomas says of Christmas, 'Love knocks with such frosted fingers' ('Blind Noel', in *No Truce with the Furies*, Bloodaxe Books, 1995).

It's cold outside. It's dark too. We're told that the shepherds, like Nicodemus, come to Jesus by night, but we do not know whether it was at night that he was born. But, as with the season, so with the hour. Night, like winter, befits his coming. The light shines in the darkness. The poets understand these things. 'While mortals sleep, the angels keep their watch of wondering love.' There is a history behind this story – Luke insists on that – but the truth of the nativity is in its poetry, not its prose. Jesus made our night-time his, as he made our winter.

Jesus is born outside and it is outsiders who find their way to him. The shepherds' home, such as it is, is the hillside, but their 'outside' status is more than a matter of where they live. Shepherds, like the silly sheep they tend, are Sabbath-breakers, and as such are condemned by the pious. The magi come to Christ out of the desert. They were never at home in their summer palaces 'with the silken girls bringing sherbet' ('The Journey of the Magi', T. S. Eliot). Matthew will contrast these pilgrim spirits with the paranoid Herod. Outside they watch the stars. Inside, he can only watch his back (Matthew 2.1–18).

Where is Christ this Christmas? Inside or outside? At St Martin-in-the-Fields we erected a Christmas crib in 'the courts of the temple', in the market by the church, where they sold boxer shorts emblazoned with the Union Jack. The curate's flat, my home for five years, overlooked this market. I looked out of my window one Christmas morning to see that, in the night, the baby Jesus had been turfed out of his crib. In his place, curled up in the straw, was a 'rough sleeper', one of London's homeless.

At midnight mass we place the figure of the newborn Christ in the crib. We welcome him into our houses of prayer. We ask Jesus in. In some of our churches his presence inside our four walls continues to be affirmed long after the crib is taken down. The gentle light in the sanctuary says, 'There he is. God is with us.' So has Christ come 'inside' at last? If he has, it is only to break down the barriers we still build, in Church and society, between the included and the excluded. The distinction between 'inside' and 'outside' was drawn when Adam was driven out of Eden. Christmas signals its destruction.

The Epiphany of the Lord

6 JANUARY

Isaiah 60.1–6; Ephesians 3.1–12; Matthew 2.1–12

WHO IS MANIFESTING CHRIST TO WHOM?

In the Uffizi Gallery in Florence there is an unfinished painting by Leonardo da Vinci depicting the Adoration of the Magi. Behind the magi, behind the child and his mother, there is ruin, confusion and conflict. Stone stairs in broken buildings lead to empty space. Distracted figures ignore the momentous event unfolding nearby. Horsemen struggle to control their terrified rearing mounts. No doubt Leonardo wishes to suggest the collapse of the pagan world, but his treatment of the story reflects Matthew's. The backdrop to the Gospel-writer's story is as dark as that drawn by the artist. A vicious tyrant rules. Innocent blood will soon be shed. Christ is born in a world awry. As at the passion of Jesus, so it is at his birth. Those in authority, both in Church and in state, dread the one who, were he to reign, would put down the mighty.

The obduracy of Jerusalem is contrasted with the openness of the East. Matthew audaciously turns a traditional theme – the haplessness of heathen quackery – on its head. Those who search the stars are more responsive to this new thing God has done than those who search the scriptures. It is as if the Egyptian magicians had outdone Joseph (Genesis 41) or Nebuchadnezzar's enchanters had got the better of Daniel (Daniel 4). T. S. Eliot, whose 'Journey of the Magi' is quoted from a thousand pulpits at Epiphany, has another account, less often cited, of the kind of characters these magi are. They are those who, 'communicate with Mars, converse with spirits, report the behaviour of the sea monster, describe the horoscope, haruspicate or scry' (Four Quartets). The first magi may have come from Persia. Today they'd set out from Glastonbury. We'd be appalled by their New Age superstitions and give them a lot of stick.

Matthew sees the magi as the first of that great company of pilgrims from all the nations who at the last day will come to yield obeisance and obedience to this child. They are the forerunners of the many who 'will come from east and west' to feast at the messianic banquet (Matthew 8.11–12). They are the first of the kings of the earth to bring their glory into the City of God (Revelation 21.24). If there are trumpets in church this Epiphany, let them sound a fanfare before the tremendous Old Testament reading. 'Nations shall come to your light, and kings to the brightness of your dawn' (Isaiah 60.3).

But – big 'but' – our triumphalism needs to be tempered.

At this season I am troubled by a memory. I took the train out of Khartoum and got off at the little village of Kubushaya. On one side of the tracks were fields and the Nile. On the other side desert and, on the horizon, crumbling pyramids. I set off for the pyramids, very foolishly, in the midday sun. The pyramids are all that is left of Meroe, the capital of biblical Ethiopia. The queen of Meroe was the 'Candace' whose steward Philip met in the desert and whom he baptized (Acts 8.26–40). To this sumptuous court, now nothing but sand and broken stones, the steward returned with the Christian gospel. I reached the pyramids and collapsed. Mercifully, out of that apparently empty desert, someone appeared. A man on a camel. He had compassion on me. All these years later I remember the love in his eyes. He put me on his own beast and brought me to an inn – or at least back to the railway station. The date was the 6th of January, the Feast of the Manifestation of Christ to the Gentiles.

There is no church in Meroe today and my Good Samaritan was a Muslim. Who on that distant day, I wonder, was manifesting Christ to whom? And as we Anglicans bicker and posture, what kind of a clouded epiphany are we offering to today's 'Gentiles'?

And what of the wise men's gifts? It is unlikely that Matthew meant each one to mean something, but of course what Matthew meant no longer matters. Matthew entrusts his marvellous story to us to make of it what we will. That is not to say that any interpretation goes. It is to insist that such an inexhaustibly suggestive story requires imaginative reading. So, yes, we may see gold as a tribute to a king, incense as a present for our great high priest, and myrrh as a grim gift for one who must suffer and die. But such interpretations are all too familiar.

I hope that one day I'll have another opportunity to produce a Christmas play I wrote long ago with the title 'The cactus, the cuckoo-clock, and the big red balloon'. The point of that frolic was to reflect laterally on an entirely serious question. 'What can *I* give him, poor as I am?'

The Presentation of Christ in the Temple

2 FEBRUARY

Malachi 3.1–5; Hebrews 2.14–18; Luke 2.22–40

UNCOMFORTING CONSOLATION

We tend to treat the *Nunc Dimittis* – Simeon's song with the infant Jesus in his arms – like a mug of Ovaltine, as a nightcap guaranteeing a good night's sleep. It's what we sing at Evensong when the day's work's done and at Compline when it's time for bed. The familiar cadences are like gentle lullabies, easing us into dreamless slumber.

'Lord, now lettest thou thy servant depart in peace.' Simeon is satisfied that all he has longed for is now fulfilled in the child in his arms. He's an old man. His life is now as light as a feather on the back of his hand and one puff of wind will blow it away ('A Song for Simeon', T. S. Eliot). Now he can contentedly take his leave in the sure knowledge that his saviour has come. As we sing his words we catch his mood and our own worries begin to drain away. All's well. We can curl up and go to sleep.

Simeon, we read, was looking forward to 'the consolation of Israel'. This term was used to describe the Messianic age. It takes up the cry by which an unnamed prophet announced his message of hope to the exiles in Babylon, 'Comfort, comfort, my people' (Isaiah 40.1). Simeon had craved that promised comfort. Now salvation is in sight, not only for his own people but for the Gentiles too. Now at last he can go to God with a serene heart.

But if our impression of Simeon himself is of a contented figure with an unequivocally comforting message, then we've mistaken our man. We have sung his song too often and with too little regard to its setting. 'The Song of Simeon' ceases to sound like soothing mood-music if we return it to its context and take account of what he actually says about the child he is holding. His words to Mary paint a darker picture. People believed that the promised 'consolation' would follow the path mapped by the prophet. Theirs would be the destiny he had foretold. They too would rise in triumph from bitter servitude. For them too the wilderness would rejoice and the desert blossom. They too would exult over their oppressors, who would watch this mighty act of God in abject awe.

Simeon foresees an altogether different fate for Israel, not a sunlit highway but the valley of the shadow of death. The end may be glorious, but the path will be a *via dolorosa*. The doom of Israel is presaged in this baby, born to be a crucified king. Simeon speaks of light and glory, but also of the 'falling' as well as the 'rising' of 'many in Israel'. It will be, as Eliot has it, 'the time of cords and scourges and lamentation'. Simeon's words anticipate what this child himself will one day say, 'The Son of Man came to give his life as a ransom for many' (Mark 10.45). For Mary herself, there is little comfort in Simeon's words. The sword, thrust into her son's side, will pierce her heart too.

Simeon turns out to be a much less reassuring figure than we have made him out to be, and 'the Presentation in the Temple' an altogether more disturbing event than we had supposed. A truer account of Simeon's meeting with the child and his mother is given by the Venetian artist Giovanni Bellini. Venice Bellini wrestled with the significance of the story of Jesus as few artists have done other than Rembrandt himself. His study of the Presentation, now in Venice's Querini Stampalia Gallery, is a great masterpiece. Looking at it, we see this scene as for the first time.

An unsmiling Simeon reaches out to take the infant Christ. We are unused to seeing babies swaddled and to us the bands, which bind him so tightly, seem like cerements. He appears to be already prepared for burial – which in a way he was. Mary seems abstracted, as if continuing to 'ponder in her heart' what had been told her concerning her child.

Two women standing by are lost in their own thoughts. One of them is turning away. Is she unaware of what unfolds beside her? Or is the burden of it too much? Joseph – it must be Joseph – stares intently, almost angrily, at us from out of the picture. He seems to say, 'Do not for one moment suppose that you understand what is happening here.'

Simeon sought consolation. But there is pain beyond consoling, as Mary found. Others, such as C. S. Lewis, have found that to be so.

> Talk to me about the truth of religion and I'll listen gladly. Talk to me about the duty of religion and I'll listen submissively. But don't come talking to me about the consolations of religion or I shall suspect that you don't understand. (*A Grief Observed*, Faber, 1961)

The Annunciation of Our Lord to the Blessed Virgin Mary

25 MARCH

Isaiah 7.10–14; Hebrews 10.4–10; Luke 1.26–38

IT IS WHAT IT IS, SAYS LOVE

The Basilica of the Annunciation in Nazareth is an immense pile. It is also a remarkably ugly building. It was built in the 1960s – the decade when many daft things were done – to replace the more modest church which previously had stood on the site. Many pilgrims feel that such a brutalist structure altogether misrepresents the unassuming and gentle woman it purports to honour. The symbol of Mary is the lily. Fittingly, the vast dome that surmounts a building that gets it all wrong is in the form of an *upside-down* lily.

Several earlier buildings preceded the present church. Neither the sumptuous Byzantine basilica nor the splendid Crusader church that succeeded it could be described as faithful in spirit to the self-effacing Mary. By the time the Crusaders arrived the Byzantine building had collapsed. In 1187 there was a particularly nasty battle between the Crusaders and the Muslims. ('Militant Muslims', we would call them today, but they were no less militant than the bloodthirsty Crusaders.)

After the battle, in which the Crusaders were defeated, the Christian inhabitants of Nazareth took refuge in the church. They were pursued into it and slaughtered. The Crusader church was sacked and razed to the ground by an emir of the Sultan of Egypt in the thirteenth century. Eventually what was left of it became a garbage tip.

The recent history of Nazareth has not testified any more clearly to the good news of the Prince of Peace. Today Nazareth's Christians fear Moslem extremism. A dispute which dragged on for years, until quashed by the Israeli authorities, centred on a provocative proposal to build a mosque next to the Basilica of the Annunciation. Nazareth, like the rest of West Bank, is under harsh occupation. The modern Jewish settlement of Nazareth, Illit, overlooking ancient Nazareth, prospers at the expense of the old city. Nazareth's Christians, looking for a future, look for it somewhere else. Some say that in a couple of generations there will be no Christians left in the city where Jesus grew up.

The story of Nazareth is a sad record of the ungodly mess we mortals have made of things. Beneath the Basilica of the Annunciation is a crypt and in the crypt is an altar and beneath the altar is an inscription. The inscription makes an absurd claim: *Verbum caro hic factum est* – 'Here the Word became flesh'. Here of all places – here where this preposterous building now stands, here where across the centuries the sons and daughters of Abraham have butchered each other and where they'd gladly do so again, here where today bewildered and exhausted tourists emerge from their air-conditioned coaches – here 'the Word became flesh'.

But there is no contradiction, no absurdity. All the holy places of the Holy Land are human places and so bear witness as much to what we do to each other as to what God has done for us. In a word, they partake of our flesh. Nazareth is as the rest. It is of the stuff which – because of Mary's 'Let it be' – the Word became.

'Let it be to me according to your word.' Mary's prayer differs from most of ours. Our prayers, at least those that well from within, rather that merely being mouthed, are more often prayers of protest rather than of acquiescence. I do not like how things are and so I post my objection. 'Let it *not* be', I plead – whether 'it' is the rain that threatens to spoil my plans for the day or the cancer that bids to take my life.

'Let it be.' Mary's acceptance of her task is rooted in her recognition that beneath all that is contradictory is an all-encompassing purpose of love. Lines written by the Austrian poet Erich Fried come to mind. Fried escaped from Vienna to England with his mother only after his father had been murdered by the Gestapo. What he witnessed and suffered lends great weight to his words.

It is madness says reason. It is what it is says love.

It is unhappiness says calculation. It is nothing but pain says fear.
It has no future says insight.

It is what it is says love.

It is ridiculous says pride. It is foolish says caution.
It is impossible says experience.

It is what it is says love.

('What it is', *100 Poems without a Country*, Calder 1987)

Perhaps those other siren voices – as well as Gabriel's – whispered in Mary's ear, the voices of calculation, fear and insight, of pride, caution and experience. If she was indeed a virgin, those voices would have been highly persuasive. But Mary accepted that it is what it is and that it is love that says so.

Where love tells me that 'it is what it is' – whatever Gabriel is asking me to do or to suffer – my prayer must be the same as Mary's 'Let it be'. How I need her to help me say it!

Ash Wednesday

Joel 2.1–2, 12–17 or Isaiah 58.1–12; 2 Corinthians 5.20b—6.10; Matthew 6.1–6, 16–21 or John 8.1–11

SAVED BY FIRE

The school of St Andrews, Turi, is spectacularly located in the highlands of Kenya's Rift Valley. From its foundation in 1931 the school was run by 'Pa' and 'Ma' Lavers, legends to this day among many old Africa hands. For years the school provided education for British 'missionary kids'. Today the school, while still Christian in its ethos, is both international and multi-cultural.

On the 29th of February 1944 a fire destroyed St Andrews. The Lavers immediately set about rebuilding the school. The symbol of St Andrew's school today is the phoenix, a mythical bird calling to mind both a brutal event and a blessed hope, both the fire that burned the school down and the faith that ashes are not the end.

After the fire Pa Lavers instituted an annual 'Phoenix Night'. On Phoenix Night each year a great bonfire is lit in the school grounds. There was a godly custom on Phoenix night, which I hope has not fallen into abeyance. Every child was invited to write on a piece of paper anything and everything in the past year that made them sad or sorry or ashamed. Then they gathered round the fire and, as a sign of their intention by God's grace to make a fresh start, they crumpled up their pieces of paper and threw them into the flames.

I don't know whether Phoenix Night at St Andrew's school ever coincided with Ash Wednesday, but what was affirmed that night resonates with what Ash Wednesday should mean for us.

On Ash Wednesday we enter what T. S. Eliot described as 'the time of tension between dying and birth'. Our purpose at this time is to rid ourselves of illusions. We pray with Eliot: 'Suffer us not to mock ourselves with falsehood.' On Ash Wednesday I hear words that the world around me conspires to drown out. As I receive on my forehead the sign of the cross, imposed in ashes, the minister says to me, 'Remember that you are dust and that to dust you shall return.' The words are said to me personally. This is not something that 'only happens to other people'. I, John Pridmore, am the one who is dust and I am the one who shall return to the dust.

The Victorians were better at facing the fact of death than we are. I do not have a skeleton by me as I say my prayers, as many a Buddhist monk does, but I do have close to hand a copy of a children's book that sold in its hundreds of thousands in the nineteenth century: Mrs Sherwood's *The History of the Fairchild Family*. Old Rogers, the Fairchild's gardener dies and the children are taken to see his body. 'You never saw a corpse, I think?' says Lucy's father. 'No, papa,' answered Lucy, 'but we have a great curiosity to see one.' Do we dislike the tale because we disapprove of what we see as a morbid preoccupation with death – or because we continue to mock ourselves and our children with falsehoods, the most mischievous of which being that you must keep young and beautiful if you want to be loved?

On Ash Wednesday I confront the reality that I am a sinner under sentence of death. But sin is not merely what individuals commit. Nor is death only what happens to sentient beings. There is social and corporate sin, the wrongs in which we are complicit by our membership of larger groups. Such groups – the crowd at a football match, the lads out together on a stag night, the nation that declares an unjust war – can behave in ways in which the men and women who form them would never do. We need to find ways of corporate repentance, ways more costly than the token apology from someone in high office.

'Dust thou art, and to dust thou shalt return.' The words said to us individually apply to our institutions too. Nobody lasts, but nothing does either. Institutions often find it hard to recognize that the time has come to let go. For example, we feel sad when a church closes, but if that church has had a useful life and has done some good then our sadness is misplaced. It looks as if the institutional church is in terminal decline, but if it is not that is not because it is immortal. Again we make Eliot's prayer our own: '*Teach us to care and not to care.*' Nothing lasts, save the love to which, as rivers to the sea, all we are and all we do returns.

On Ash Wednesday we face reality. We face our own sinfulness and mortality and that of the fleeting show of things, our religious structures included. And – very deliberately – we turn. We repent. We draw near to God and – like boys and girls throwing balls of crunched-up paper into a bonfire – we ask that all that is ill in us may be consumed in the inextinguishable fire of his love.

Monday of Holy Week

Isaiah 42.1–9; Hebrews 9.11–15; John 12.1–11

THE GENTLE WAY OF THE CROSS

There are many paths to the cross. Our readings for Holy Week provide one such path. These scriptures lead us to Calvary. Today, and on Tuesday and Wednesday, we are invited to consider one who, like Jesus, comes to us as one unknown. The pattern of his life too was cruciform. He is the subject of a series of poems, written four centuries or more before the time of Jesus, to be found in the later chapters of the book of Isaiah. Often he is just called 'the servant' and the poems that speak of him simply described as 'the servant songs'.

Today we read the first of these 'servant songs'. God delights, we read, in his servant. He describes what his servant will do. The servant's purpose, we read, is to bring 'justice to the nations'. In the Hebrew Bible, justice is not so much what is secured by an impartial judicial process. It is, rather, the result of God's action to save the vulnerable and oppressed.

When Jesus of Nazareth sets out on his mission he makes the servant's programme his own. In the synagogue at Nazareth, Jesus announces that he will fulfil the servant's role by bringing good news to those who rarely hear good news, namely the poor, by restoring sight to the blind and by liberating the enslaved (Luke 4.16–21).

What is remarkable about the servant is the way he works. The servant's method, which will be Christ's method, is not the means by which most would-be liberators operate. The servant's way is not an exercise of power but a display of gentleness – even of weakness. Certainly it will look like weakness to those watching. It is, in a word, the way of the cross.

The servant does not 'cry or lift up his voice, or make it heard in the street'. Nor does Jesus as, bearing his cross, he makes his painful way from the Antonia Fortress, where Pilate has condemned him to crucifixion, to the killing field outside the city where the execution will take place.

The servant's way will always be Christ's way. It is 'not to break bruised reeds'. The Christ, who is so like the servant, does not impose yet greater burdens on those already near breaking point. So it must be for those who seek to serve the servant Christ. The disciples of Jesus, says Paul, are to be known for their master's gentleness (Philippians 4.5). The implications of the principle of 'not breaking bruised reeds' are far-reaching. To begin near home, the Church that preaches this Biblical ethic would do so more persuasively if it did not overload its own clergy so badly. Maybe it is right to ask the Christian minister to go the extra mile, but not if you have already broken his back.

The servant does not quench 'the dimly burning wick'. Nor does the servant of Christ. It is easy to snuff out a feeble flame, whether that flame be some first stumbling step of faith or a tentative attempt to lead a better life.

Our readings in Holy Week are chosen, first, to bring us closer to the cross and, second, to guide us on the path of the cross which will be our pilgrims' way until our life's end. We ask what it is about 'the servant' that determines Jesus's understanding of his mission and that must shape our own discipleship. This at least we learn from the servant and from Christ: that in worlds as harsh as ours, their way was gentle. Which gentleness we crave.

We are directed to the servant songs in Holy Week. We are sent too to John's Gospel. Today we watch and ponder the gentleness of Jesus towards Mary whose extravagance and outrageous conduct incensed Judas and – if the parallel Gospel stories are anything to go by (Matthew 26.6–13, Mark 14.3–9) – angered others present too.

But we notice Lazarus as well. Lazarus, recently exhumed and brought back to life, is an object of macabre fascination. For some, their fascination has turned into faith, faith in the one who has made good his claim to be the resurrection and the life. For others, Lazarus back from the dead is a threat they must eliminate. They realize that there cannot be a stronger sign that Jesus is who he says he is than having someone lately a corpse walking around for all to see.

We read that 'they planned to put Lazarus to death as well as Jesus'. Did they succeed in doing so? History does not tell us, but they may well have done. Again, we are bound to reflect what a mixed blessing it was for Lazarus to be restored to life. Lazarus's death and resurrection were his baptism, his participation in the dying and rising of Jesus. All of us, when we are baptized, are set free from our grave-cloths to become Christ's soldiers and servants to our lives' end. For Lazarus, that end probably came soon enough.

Tuesday of Holy Week

Isaiah 49.1–7; 1 Corinthians 1.18–31; John 12.20–36

THE BROKEN KING

In the closing pages of T. H. White's magisterial reworking of the Arthurian myths, *The Once and Future King* (Collins, 1958), we have an almost unbearably moving portrait of a broken king. Arthur concludes that his life's work has been wasted. He had sought to build the better world he believed in, a round table, not only for his knights but for the nations. Now at the end, as he surveys the wreckage of his hopes, he is near despair. 'Justice had been his last attempt – to do nothing which was not just. But it had ended in failure. To do at all had proved too difficult. He was done himself.'

The mysterious central figure of the prophetic poems we call 'the servant songs' is overwhelmed by the same sense of failure. He laments that he has 'laboured in vain'. Is he nearing the end of his life? Clearly he is at the end of his tether. The servant wonders what his life amounts to. He concludes that the sum of his efforts has been 'for nothing and vanity', an appraisal as bleak as that later written across all human endeavour, 'All is vanity and a striving after wind' (Ecclesiastes 1.14).

The broken king and the despairing servant are very close. Both sought justice and both refused to accept that justice can be secured only by beating your enemies in bloody combat. Justice is not justice if imposed forcibly by the victors on the vanquished. Neither Arthur nor the servant will break the bruised reed or quench the dimly burning wick.

On the way of the cross you never seem to win. You never *seem* to win. Those who follow that path will often be tempted to suppose that how things look is how things are and how they always will be. Like the servant, like Arthur, like Christ at his darkest hour on his cross, they will feel themselves defeated. Many ministers, looking back across a lifetime's labours, share Peter's feelings: 'Master, we have worked all night long but have caught nothing' (Luke 5.5).

The servant believes that he has failed in the mission to which he was called before he was born. The goal of that mission was to bring Israel back to God. God's response to his servant's confession of failure is not to condemn him, but neither is it to ask less of him. He does not reduce the servant's role; he extends it. Bringing Israel home to God is too light a task. The servant must look beyond Israel. The servant's mission must now be universal. He is to be 'a light to the nations'.

Like the servant, Jesus accepts that he has a wider mission than to the house of Israel. According to John, confirmation comes to Jesus that he is to be 'light to the nations' and the bearer of God's salvation 'to the ends of the earth', when he hears that 'some Greeks' are seeking to see him. The Gentiles' wish to see him is the indication Jesus has been waiting for, the sign that his hour has come. This will not be the hour for Israel's oppressors to be defeated in battle and for power and prosperity to be restored to God's subjugated people. It will be the hour when the grain of wheat falls into the ground and dies. It will be the hour when Jesus will perfectly fulfil the mission of the servant. Like the servant, he will be despised and rejected, afflicted and crushed. Like the servant, he will bear in his own body the infirmities and iniquities of humankind (Isaiah 52.13–53.12). Paradoxically, this will be the hour when he, the Son of Man, will be 'glorified'.

But at this very moment, Jesus – like Arthur, like the suffering servant – wonders whether his mission has failed. At the moment when he embraces the servant's role and all it will entail, his faith is overtaken by doubt. 'What should I say,' asks Jesus, '"Father, save me from this hour?"' According to John, Gethsemane is still to come but already Jesus is suffering its anguish. Acute spiritual distress has physical symptoms. Luke famously refers to Jesus sweating great drops of blood (Luke 22.44). T. H. White's description of Arthur's anguish before his last battle could be read as a commentary on Jesus's Gethsemane of spirit and body as he faces the cross: 'He felt as if there were something atrophied between his eyes, where the base of the nose grew into the skull.'

Jesus found himself in a dark place as he contemplated what faced him. I must register what he says about that place, if I dare. 'Where I am, there will my servant be also.' I shall find myself in that place too, it seems, if I am a Christian – and if I never find myself there it may be because I am something else.

Wednesday of Holy Week

Isaiah 50.4–9a; Hebrews 12.1–3; John 13.21–32

WHERE THE BUCK STOPS

Once more we look to 'the servant', to the one who – so said the prophet-poet – would suffer to set God's people free. The prophet hears the servant speak: 'I gave my back to those who struck me.' The servant lets them do their worst to him. So does Jesus. He absorbs all that shames us – not least our anger, the anger that one social commentator tells us is 'the defining characteristic of our times'.

I think of Michael. Michael was a huge small child, a morbidly obese ten-year-old, in a children's club I ran when I was a curate. Michael was desperate for love but he didn't get much, because he didn't smell nice. One winter's evening, as the kids were going home, Michael was in a terrible state, in floods of tears, shuddering with grief. He'd lost a coin, presumably fallen from his pocket. I see Michael now at the door of the church hall. There was bicycle there, leaning against the wall. Michael noticed it. Suddenly he stopped sobbing. He reached out and wrenched the front lamp from the bike. He switched the lamp on and shone its beam into the night sky. Then he shouted angrily up into the darkness: 'It's all your fault! You up there! It's all your bloody fault!'

Michael knew where the buck must stop. He turned to the crucified God to absorb and quench his anger. As we all must, unless we want those bush fires in our belly to burn for ever.

The servant continues, 'I did not hide my face from insult and spitting.' We are invited in our second reading to 'consider him who endured such hostility against himself from sinners'. The writers use past tenses, talking as if the suffering is done with. But today we ask whether Christ's face is still exposed to our insults, whether to this day he endures our enmity and anger.

Peter Abelard was one of the great Christian theologians of the middle-ages. He held the world in his hands. But because of his love for Heloise and what that had led to, he was a broken man. The novelist Helen Waddell tells a story about him. Abelard was surviving in the forest with his one servant, Thibault. One day they hear a terrible screaming. At first they fear it is a child. They rush to where the screams are coming from – and find that it is a rabbit caught in a trap. Abelard releases the rabbit and it dies in his arms. It's all too much for him. 'I've deserved all I've suffered. But what did this one do? Is there a God at all?'

Thibault notices nearby a tree that has been felled. Its trunk has been sawn through, exposing all the growth rings. 'Look,' says Thibault, 'that dark ring there. It runs the whole length of the tree. But you only see it where it is cut across. Perhaps Calvary is like that. It is the bit of God we see. But it goes on.'

It goes on. There *is* a cross – present tense – in the heart of God.

In our Gospel, we hear how Judas Iscariot left the upper room, intent on betraying Jesus. Why did Judas betray Jesus? Perhaps there was anger there, anger that Jesus had not proved the kind of Messiah that Judas had hoped he would be. If so, there is much of Judas in most of us. Like Judas, we have asked great things of God but our prayers have not been answered, and we are angry too. Our anger still burns, however piously we pretend otherwise. Better to let that anger out and to direct it towards the one place – we shall reach it on Good Friday – where it can be extinguished.

Jesus Christ, the suffering servant, still gives his back to those who strike him. The First World War army chaplain Studdert Kennedy witnessed men being slaughtered like cattle. That experience blew to bits his complacent faith in a God somehow above it all, untouched by our misery. There in the trenches he became convinced that if Christ's passion tells us anything, it tells us what God *is* like.

Father, if he, the Christ, were thy revealer,
Truly the first begotten of the Lord,
Then must thou be a suff'rer and a healer,
Pierced to the heart by the sorrow of the sword.

Then must it mean, not only that thy sorrow
Smote thee that once upon the lonely tree,

But that today, tonight, and on the morrow,
Still it will come, O Gallant God, to thee.
('The Suffering God')

One word more about Judas Iscariot. John does not resolve the paradox of Judas. Satan has 'entered' Judas and he does what Satan requires of him. But what Satan requires of Judas is also what Jesus tells him to do. If Judas was angry, that was not the whole story. That story is unfinished and its loose ends remain. Better to live with the loose ends than to try to tie them up too soon.

Maundy Thursday

Exodus 12.1–4 (5–10), 11–14; 1 Corinthians 11.23–26; John 13.1–17, 31b–35

GETTING DOWN

On the 5th July 1941 the troopship HMS Anselm was struck by a torpedo. The torpedo hit the hold on C deck where scores of men were sleeping. The hold swiftly began filling with water. The ship was soon listing. At any moment it might sink. The stairway had been blown away. There was no means of escape for all those trapped. At the entrance above, a man in a dressing gown joined the others looking down into the hold. He asked to be lowered into the hold. They tried to dissuade him, but he insisted. He said that he must be with his men. His name was Herbert Pugh. He was an airforce chaplain. So they lowered him into the hold. Those above saw him praying with the doomed men. Then they fled to the boats. Moments later the ship plunged and sank. Herbert Pugh was awarded, posthumously, the George Cross.

One image from that story has stayed with me since I first heard it – the image of one who chose to go down into dark waters and to let those waters engulf him. Jesus chose to do that when he was baptized. He sealed that choice on the first Maundy Thursday, when he refused a last chance to save himself, when he consented to go down into the dark waters of our sins and our sorrows and to let those waters close over him.

In Holy Week we are with Jesus on his journey. That journey began long before Palm Sunday; long before he began his ministry; long before he was born or conceived. The journey of Jesus began in the heart of God before time began. From all eternity, God was in Christ on his way to win us back to himself. 'Love came down at Christmas' – yes, but that love was coming down all along. That is what love does. Love comes down. That is love's trajectory.

Tonight we watch one moment on the journey that began in the heart of God. Jesus gets down. All along, that has been the direction of his journey; the journey that took him from his father's side, the journey that brought him to our broken earth, the journey that brought him to birth at Bethlehem, the journey that dragged him down beneath those lethal waters at his baptism, the journey that led him to Jerusalem, the journey that brings him tonight to a dirty floor, where dogs scavenge for scraps, where slaves kneel to wash filthy feet.

Jesus gets down. That descent, says St Paul, must shape our mind-set. 'Let the same mind be in you', he says, 'that was in Jesus Christ, who . . . emptied himself, became a slave, was born like us, humbled himself, suffered death, death on the cross' (Philippians 2.5–8). Jesus gets down. It is the Christian 'feng shui'. It determines the orientation of the disciple's life. It is the way we are meant to live now – in the little time left before all comes to its appointed end.

John, and only John, tells the story of how Jesus washes his disciples' feet. For John, the story is very simple. 'I have set you an example,' says Jesus. 'You should do as I have done.' Words of one syllable. What I have done, you must do.

On Maundy Thursday I am moved by the memory of someone who took Jesus at his word. I had landed at an airport somewhere in Africa. I was there to visit some missionaries. I was tired after a long flight and I was irritated that there was no one at the airport to meet me. So I resigned myself to having to make my own way into town. A scruffy and clearly impoverished porter seized my heavy and expensive suitcases and staggered off towards a row of clapped-out taxis. I hurried after him, still fuming that I hadn't been met. When we got to the taxi rank my scruffy porter, still humping my bags, introduced himself. He was the diocesan bishop. Thank God, I didn't try to tip him.

Tonight's great gift is not 'Maundy money', but a new mandate. Not an eleventh commandment, but a single commandment, which, if only we could begin to keep it, would do away with the other ten for good. 'Love one another,' says Jesus, 'just as I have loved you'.

Jesus gets down, as we must. To be sure, that descent is not the end. Very soon we shall be singing, 'Up from the grave he arose'. There is

Easter Day and Ascension Day and the New Testament promises that we are to be with him on those stages of his journey too. 'We will certainly be united with him in a resurrection like his', says St Paul (Romans 6.5). But one day at a time. We are not there yet. The cross, to which we are so close tonight, comes before the crown.

Good Friday

Isaiah 52.13—53.12; Hebrews 10.16–25 or 4.14–16; 5.7–9; John 18.1—19.42

CHRIST'S CROSS AND OURS

I was a school chaplain for many years. I used to try to explain to my confirmation classes what the cross means. We'd all sit on cushions on the floor at a big round low table with a white surface. And I'd give everyone a water-based felt-tip pen, a 'magic marker'. Then I'd invite these young people to write all over the table, to write down anything and everything that made them unhappy or ashamed about their world or, if they wanted to, about their own lives. Then I would ask them to imagine that table as being as big as the big round world – indeed as being so vast that it reached from the beginning to the end of time.

Then I would invite them to think of all they had written on the table as funnelling in, as coming together and bearing down, on one point at the very centre of the table. And then I would place, there at the centre of the table, a simple wooden cross.

And so we thought of Christ's cross, there at the midpoint of history, there in the midst of the mess we have made of things. We would picture that crucified figure, absorbing the shame and the pain of all we had written, taking into himself all the ills that were and are and will be. We thought of that one lonely figure carrying – and carrying away – all the sins and sorrows of our sad human story.

Then we would wipe the table clean.

Christ on his cross absorbs all that shames us – including our anger, the anger that poisons the wells of our being. Christopher Nolan, who died on the 20th February 2009, suffered from severe cerebral palsy, but he was also a successful poet, novelist and playwright. His book *Under the Eye of the Clock* won the Whitbread Prize. Every word he wrote was tapped out on a typewriter with a pointer strapped to his forehead.

Christopher Nolan's obituary in the *Guardian* contained this paragraph:

> One American journalist insinuated that Nolan had a ghost writer. Disgusted, brooding, Nolan asked his father, while they were out together, to take him inside a church. In front of a life-size crucifix, Nolan swung his left arm in a two-fingered gesture. He felt better for that and then, on a much-needed holiday at Great Skellig, he forgave the journalist – and his Maker.

What happened on Good Friday? I look to the Scottish writer George MacDonald to help me understand. In one of his novels George MacDonald tells the story of a violently abused child. Gibbie is a sweet child, but he is deaf and dumb. This silent child is in the service of a cruel laird. One day the laird takes a horsewhip to Gibbie. He inflicts two dreadful lashes on the boy's back. Gibbie runs away. He flees into the mountains. A woman, Janet, a shepherd's wife, sees the bleeding child stumbling across the hillside.

> With a horror of pitiful amazement, Janet saw a great cross marked in two cruel stripes on his back . . . Could it be (she thought) that the Lord was still, child and man, suffering for his race, to deliver his brothers and sisters from their sins? – wandering, enduring, beaten, blessing still? Accepting the evil, slaying it, and returning none? His patience the one rock where the evil word finds no echo; his heart the one gulf into which the dead-sea wave rushes with no recoil . . . the one abyss of destroying love, into which all wrong tumbles, and finding no reaction, is lost, ceases forevermore . . .

Six words strike me: 'the one abyss of destroying love'. The cross is the place where our anger is quenched, our anger with ourselves, with others and with God. Golgotha is the gulf which consumes all our woes and wickedness *without recoil*.

Four hundred years before the time of Jesus a prophet, who was also a poet, spoke of a 'servant' who would one day suffer to set God's people free. This servant, the prophet said, would bear the people's sins and share their sorrows. And he would do so – like George Macdonald's Gibbie – *silently*. 'He was led like a lamb to the slaughter, and as a sheep before her shearers is dumb, *so he did not open his mouth*.'

Golgotha is the gulf which consumes our woes. In John Bunyan's *Pilgrim's Progress*, Bunyan dreams of how Christian, bearing a heavy burden on his back, comes to a cross on a little hill. At the foot of the hill is a sepulchre. Bunyan writes:

> So I saw in my dream, that just as Christian came to the cross, his burden loosed from off his shoulders, and fell from off his back, and began to tumble, and so continued to do till it came to the mouth of the sepulchre, where it fell in, and I saw it no more.

And Bunyan adds, 'Then Christian gave three leaps for joy, and went on singing.'

Easter Eve

Job 14.1–14 or Lamentations 3.1–9, 19–24; 1 Peter 4.1–8; Matthew 27.57–66 or John 19.38–42

TOUCHING THE ROCK

Calvary stands in many places. Wherever in the world sin and suffering have carved deep wounds, those wounds are in the shape of a cross. I think of 'the Gulag Archipelago', the chain of labour camps across Siberia to which the Soviet government consigned those they deemed enemies of the state. Millions perished there. Calvary stood in the Gulag Archipelago.

The Russian writer Alexander Solzhenitsyn, one of the towering moral and spiritual giants of modern times, was a prisoner in the Gulag. In his great book *The Gulag Archipelago* he writes of his time there. He tells how those camps robbed him of everything that makes life meaningful. He is robbed of his name – he is known only by a number. He is robbed of books, pen and paper – a dreadful deprivation for a writer of his stature. He is robbed of work he can do with dignity. Instead he must labour as a slave. He is deprived of sufficient food and sleep. He gets no letters. He hears no news of his family or of the outside world. He is stripped of his own clothes and dressed in rags. He is robbed of his health – he succumbs to cancer.

Solzhenitsyn, robbed of everything, sinks as it were to the bottom, to the very base of being. And then he says something extraordinary. He writes of the day, 'when I deliberately let myself sink to the bottom *and felt it firm under my feet* – the hard rocky bottom which is the same for all'.

St Paul writes of Christ's descent into the depths.

> And being found in appearance as a man, he humbled himself and became obedient to death – even death on a cross. (Philippians 2.7–8)

'Even death on a cross.' On Holy Saturday we reflect that even that, perhaps, was not the limit of his descent. He was brought lower still. As the Apostles' Creed has it, 'He descended into hell.' Some modern versions of the creed, nervous of the notion of Jesus in hell, have a different turn of phrase. 'He descended', the translators say, 'to the place of the departed.' The point is, they say, that Jesus truly died. His death was not a charade. True enough, but that talk of hell was saying something about the death of Jesus which we need to hear. It is saying that Jesus went somewhere worse than where what he endured in his body brought him. Beyond what Christ suffered in his flesh, there was what has been called 'the inner crucifixion' of Christ, what he suffered in heart and mind and spirit. Where did that 'inner crucifixion' bring him? How do you describe that place? All words fail, but the word 'hell' fails less than some.

For some, the story of this day, when Christ has gone into the dark, is the story of their lives. This night of darkness lasts their lifetime. They somehow never quite make it to Easter Day.

The poet Gerard Manley Hopkins wrote glorious joyful poetry. 'Glory be to God for dappled things!' ('Pied Beauty') he sang. But for Hopkins, for much of the time, it was inwardly dark. 'I wake and feel the fell of dark, not day', he wrote.

What can we do if we find ourselves in such darkness? I find it helpful to keep on saying just six words from the Psalms: 'He made darkness his secret place' (Psalm 18.11). God is there, says the Psalmist, even if 'I make my bed in hell' (Psalm 139.8).

The traditional site of the crucifixion is in the Church of the Holy Sepulchre. To reach the very place where they say Jesus died, you enter the church, turn right and go up a short flight of stairs. You find yourself in a small chapel. There are icons and lots of candles. Against one wall is an altar, standing, it is said, over the exact point where the cross stood. Under the altar is a small hole in the floor of the chapel. Many pilgrims come here to say their prayers. If you do what most of these pilgrims do, you will kneel before the altar, reach beneath it, and put your hand through that hole. If you do so, you will find yourself touching the rough hard cold surface of a bare rock.

Tonight, in imagination, we join those pilgrims in the Church of the Holy Sepulchre. In our minds, we kneel with them before that altar. With them we reach down to touch that rock.

Perhaps if we do that we shall catch a sense of something that our stupid words cannot begin to explain, a sense of what lies beneath all the confusions and contradictions of our mixed-up lives. Perhaps we shall 'touch the rock', the same rock that Christ touched in the dark place he went to for us.

So may we find, as our Saviour did, that 'the eternal God is our refuge and underneath are the everlasting arms' (Deuteronomy 33.27).

Ascension Day

Acts 1.1–11 or Daniel 7.9–14; Ephesians 1.15–23 or Acts 1.1–11; Luke 24.44–53

ALL WE ARE IS WHAT HE IS

I have no difficulty in believing that twelve men climbed a mountain, and that, having reached the summit, one of them carried on climbing. It is no problem to me that the last sight his companions had of him – as depicted subsequently in many a stained-glass window – was of two feet disappearing into a cloud. I am untroubled by the claim that at that point two other men, in long white coats, appeared from nowhere to reassure the bewildered eleven that their friend would return in due course in the same surprising way that he left them.

What bothers me, what I find far harder to believe than this strange tale of self-levitation, is what the story has been taken to mean. St Paul steered subsequent interpretation of the Ascension with what we hear in our reading from his letter to the Ephesians. 'God has seated Christ at his right hand,' Paul writes. Jesus the suffering servant has become Christ the triumphant warrior. He is *Christus Victor*, back from his battlefield, all his enemies slaughtered. He does not hang from a cross, but sits on a throne. There he sits and there he stays. There will be no further need for him to get to his feet, for the conquest of his foes is complete. That is what I find hard to believe.

Paul's triumphalist tones are sounded in our traditional ascension hymns. Some of the cruder seasonal effusions have been dropped from our hymnals, but there are many much-loved old numbers, abounding in their 'Alleluias' and steeped in their Pauline theology, that we still sing.

Hail the day that sees him rise
To his throne above the skies
Christ the lamb for sinners slain
Enters now the highest heaven

There for him high triumph waits
Lift your heads, eternal gates
He hath conquered death and sin
Take the king of glory in.

Christ has conquered death and sin. This is a thrilling thought and the songs in which we voice it are appropriately rousing. The problem is that we cannot sing such words with conviction and enthusiasm if we are distracted by what is going on in the world outside the church whose roof we are raising, a world where sin and death and unspeakable suffering show few signs of defeat.

Shortly after the First World War, the army chaplain and poet G. A. Studdert Kennedy published a series of meditations on the Apostles' Creed for which he found a fine title (*Food for the Fed-up*, Hodder and Stoughton, 1921). What 'Woodbine Willie', as the soldiers affectionately called him, said about the creed was shaped by the unspeakable carnage he witnessed on the Western Front. When he saw soldiers drowning in mud he found words about Jesus soaring into the sky sticking in his throat.

'He ascended into heaven.' Studdert Kennedy begins his discussion of this implausible claim with the tersest of questions – 'Did he?' 'O my God,' he writes, 'these tales of unbearable beauty that break the hearts of men because they are not true! I came out of Birmingham Cathedral, from the Burne-Jones window of the Ascension, into the twilight streets and a prostitute giggled.'

The traditional interpretation of the Ascension focuses on the story as the dramatic sign of Christ's victory. Despite appearances to the contrary, Satan is done for. The Ascension, so understood, is seen as the *coup de grâce*, the final blow with which the devil's power is destroyed. What if the whole of history seems to contradict this claim? Christians will still patiently insist that the whole of history is not the end of history and that ultimately God will win.

But there is another way to take the story, a view of the ascension that perhaps will speak more powerfully to our twenty-first-century despair as we watch the triumph of iniquity in the world and in our own flesh.

It is, in fact, what the Christian Church has always taught about this strangest of stories. To say that Christ is ascended is to affirm that the humanity which God assumed by his incarnation is for ever his. Our flawed human nature was not, as it were, a suit of clothes which God in Christ put on for thirty years or so, an outfit which he then discarded when he went back to heaven. The ascended Christ is still one of us. All we are – much of it so wretched – is what he is.

As Archbishop Rowan Williams has said, in a memorable sermon preached in Canterbury Cathedral, 'Our humanity in all its variety, in all its vulnerability, has been taken by Jesus into the heart of the divine life . . . the humanity that we all know to be stained, wounded, imprisoned in various ways; this humanity – yours and mine – is still capable of being embraced by God, shot through with God's glory, received and welcomed in the burning heart of reality itself.'

All Saints' Day

1 NOVEMBER

Isaiah 56.3–8 or 2 Esdras 2.42–48; Hebrews 12.18–24; Matthew 5.1–12

All Saints Day sends us to scripture, sacred and secular. Graham Greene's *The Power and the Glory* (Heinemann, 1940) belongs to the canon of secular scripture, those writings – not in the Bible – which help us walk the way of Christ. It is the story of a worldly 'whisky priest', who is being hunted down in an anti-clerical purge in Mexico in the 30s. This pathetic figure is 'too human for heroism, too humble for martyrdom', yet in the end Christ's Calvary and his are one. As he wakes at dawn on the day he is to be shot, he is possessed by one conviction. 'He knew now that at the end there was only one thing that mattered – to be a saint.'

Nothing else matters but to be a saint.

Who are the saints? There are of course the saints whom the church has officially recognized. My favourite is the founder of the Salesians, Saint Don Bosco, the patron saint of conjurers, who taught by love and magic. After Mass in his village church, Don Bosco would gather the children of the poor around him and tell them Bible stories, illustrating them by juggling and sleight of hand. St Don Bosco is important because he shows that the quest for sanctity, while always a serious business, can still be fun. He amply meets the description of a saint as 'someone who makes goodness attractive'.

Don Bosco was a Roman Catholic canonized by a Pope. In other Christian traditions, we do not formally honour the memory of exceptionally holy people in this way, nor do we claim – though we do not disclaim the possibility – that their prayers can be invoked on our behalf. For example, a couple of days before All Saints Day, the Church of England invites us to remember the missionary James Hannington, who gave his name to a lake and his life for the Gospel.

We praise God 'for all the saints who from their labours rest'. Some of those saints resting from their labours are famous, even if we know next to nothing about them. But the vast majority of the saints who await their glorious resurrection remain unsung. In a society which fawns on celebrities, in which merely to be known matters much more than being known for anything in particular, it is important that we deliberately give thanks for those hidden and forgotten saints. The saints who sustain local communities or churches rarely sit on their councils – although some saints, much to their reluctance, end up on them.

All Saints Day sends us to sacred scripture. In the strange text with which our Bible closes, John records a vision granted to him of a great multitude of the saints around the throne of the Lamb of God (Revelation 7.9–17). His account includes an interesting exchange. One of the celestial sidesmen asks John who these white-robed figures are. John's reply – 'Sir, you know' – amounts to an admission of his ignorance. John cannot explain what it is to be a saint. Nor can we. We talk about 'the problem of evil'. Goodness is equally perplexing. At its simplest, it is the baffling question, 'Why is she so nice, when I'm so nasty?' On All Saints Day we praise the God we cannot explain for the saints we cannot explain.

Saints come to mind as we read the Beatitudes and the Beatitudes come to mind as we think of the saints. Pier Giorgio Frassati was a wealthy young man from Turin who was dedicated to social action on behalf of the poor and marginalized. He was often heard to say, 'Charity is not enough; we need social reform.' He died of polio at the age of 24. The story of his life and death influenced the young Karol Wojtyla, who, as Pope John Paul II, described Frassati as 'a man of the eight Beatitudes'.

A saint is 'a man, a woman, or a child of the eight Beatitudes'. If so, the Beatitudes are not distinct and separate criteria. A saint isn't someone who can, as it were, tick all eight boxes. All the Beatitudes are contained in each of them and each of them embraces the rest. Søren Kierkegaard's exposition of the sixth Beatitude, *Purity of Heart is to Will One Thing*, is a commentary on them all. The saints – though this is not to explain them – are those who 'will one thing', who are undivided in their intentions. That is why Grahame Greene's picture of the 'whisky priest', who came to see that 'there was only one thing that mattered', is a study of sanctity.

The single-minded quest for sanctity is probably easier for monks and nuns than for those 'in the world'. It's hard to 'will one thing' when you are struggling to cope with the multiple commitments of home and work – not to speak of pulling your weight on the PCC. But you'll still sometimes glimpse a saint on the 8.27 from Surbiton.

FESTIVALS

The Naming and Circumcision of Jesus

1 JANUARY

Numbers 6.22–27; Galatians 4.4–7 or Philippians 2.5–11; Luke 2.15–21

NAMED AND WOUNDED

The atheist philosopher A. C. Grayling recently wrote a characteristically combative article in the *New Statesman* entitled 'The Empty Name of God' (*New Statesman*, 9 April 2009). Grayling holds that 'the basic doctrines of the major religions have their roots in the superstitions and fancies of illiterate peasants living several thousand years ago'. The claim, too silly even to amount to a mistake, does not merit attention. But it is worth pausing on Grayling's title, especially on the day when we consider the name of the one we call both Lord and God. Because of course Grayling is, in a way, right.

In Hebrew thinking, someone's name tells you what you need to know about them. The Hebrew Bible, our Old Testament, abounds with names with significant meanings. Abraham is 'the father of a multitude' (Genesis 17.5), Isaac is a cause of 'laughter' – at least, the prediction of his birth was (Genesis 21.1–7), Jacob is 'the supplanter' (Genesis 27.36), and so on. Such names tell you something of the story of those who bear them. Names with meanings can also be names with messages. The prophet Isaiah saddled two of his children with names which must have embarrassed them in the playground: Shearjashub ('a remnant shall return') and Maher-shalal-hash-baz ('pillage hastens; looting speeds'). Children with such names were signs of what God had in store for his people. Thanks be to God, another son was born to Isaiah whose name was less ambiguous and threatening: Immanuel 'God with us' (Isaiah 7.3, 14; 8.3).

Biblical names are far from empty – except, that is, for God's name. When the Bible tells me someone's name, I can, as it were, say to them, 'Now I know who you are!' But when the Bible tells me God's name, I cannot say the same to him. I ask God who he is and the answer he gives me is the same he gave to Moses at the burning bush. 'I AM WHO I AM' (Exodus 3.14). Moses was none the wiser. Nor am I.

So when Grayling talks about 'the empty name of God' he is talking more truly than he knows. Names represent. We cannot represent God. Any representation would be an idol. God's name is, in that sense, 'empty', just as the Holy of Holies in the Temple at Jerusalem was empty. If I name someone, I identify them and secure a purchase on them. It's what Adam did to the animals (Genesis 2.20). I cannot do that to God.

What of the name of Jesus? The name 'Jesus' means 'God saves' (Matthew 1.21). What was not made known about God in the name revealed to Moses is made known in the name Jesus.

But there is more to his name. Paul speaks of the exaltation of Jesus, through and beyond the cross, when God gave him 'the name that is above every name'. That name is the name Jesus, at which 'every knee shall bow'. But it is also the name beyond all names. 'Every tongue shall confess that Jesus Christ is Lord', says Paul, taking up the cry and the claim of the first Christians. The title 'Lord' is the term that has always been substituted for God's name YHWH – a word with no vowels, for it will never be spoken (Philippians 2.5–11). That ineffable name is also his. Who then is Jesus? He too is Who He Is.

The ladies of Victorian vicarages tended to be ill for much of the time and to write a lot of hymns. Caroline Noel, the invalid daughter of a London clergyman, published a collection of hymns under the title *The Name of Jesus and Other Poems for the Sick and Lonely*. The hymn 'At the Name of Jesus, every knee shall bow' first appeared in this collection. It strikes one as a remarkably hearty hymn coming from someone so fragile, especially if it is sung, as it usually is, to the bouncy tune by Michael Brierley. That said, the words of the hymn express the New Testament theology of the name of Jesus accurately, clearly and powerfully. One verse in particular is a remarkable example of how much can be well said in brief compass.

Name him, brothers, name him,
with love as strong as death,
but with awe and wonder
and with bated breath;
he is God the Saviour,
he is Christ the Lord,
ever to be worshiped,
trusted, and adored.

Editors of modern hymn-books have to do something with the first line, but there is no need to tinker with the rest. What I take to heart is

Caroline Noel's perception that, if what the Bible says about the name of Jesus is true, I should be careful how I use it.

Today's festival is both of the naming and of the circumcision of Jesus. If we are not too squeamish, we can make the connections. His role, revealed in his name, is revealed too as the knife draws blood. Only eight days old, he is already being wounded for our transgressions.

The Conversion of Paul

25 JANUARY

Jeremiah 1.4–10 or Acts 9.1–22; Acts 9.1–22 or Galatians 1.11–16a; Matthew 19.27–30

NO END TO THE DAMASCUS ROAD

As a boy, I was taught that to become a Christian you had to be 'converted' – better still, 'gloriously converted'. I was also told that, if I was a Christian, I must be prepared, if called on, to stand up and to 'give my testimony'. Your 'testimony' was your account of your conversion. Your testimony carried greater weight if it included a graphic description of a conspicuously sinful past. Testimonies of this order have always constituted a powerful form of Christian apologetic. Those of us whose sins have only been the usual boring ones have been much at a disadvantage when giving our testimonies. The present writer will always be upstaged by his namesake, the famous Roman Catholic evangelist John Pridmore, formerly 'a notorious East End face'.

Paul was not converted. At least his conversion was not an event, such as might take place at an evangelistic rally. His conversion was a lifelong process, as the journey of all who turn to God, by whatever name they know him, must always be. Saul, as he was first called, was brought up in the Jewish faith. He was a student of the eminent Rabbi Gamaliel. He attended synagogue. He zealously observed the Jewish law. The impact on Paul – and on human history – of his experience on the Damascus road was momentous, but it is altogether misleading to understand it as his conversion to Christianity. In the light – both blinding and illuminating – of that experience he was led to a radical reinterpretation of his Jewish faith, but it would be the crudest of errors to suppose that when he left Jerusalem he was a Jew but by the time he had reached Damascus he had become a Christian.

To be sure, Paul changed his mind about Jesus. Jesus had appeared to him. That 'appearance' was overwhelming. It profits us not at all to probe into the nature of that appearance, save to say that Paul himself saw it as comparable to the 'appearances' of Jesus to his followers subsequent to his crucifixion (1 Corinthians 15.1–11). What was now incontrovertibly evident to Paul was that he had been wrong in persecuting those – all of them, as he was, observant Jews – who had seen in Jesus the fulfilment of the hopes of Israel. So he accepted baptism into 'the Jesus movement', one movement among many others within first-century Judaism.

Paul's acceptance of what the first followers of Jesus claimed about him leads him – it is all part of Paul's continuing conversion – to conclude that the story of Jesus is good news for Gentile as well as for Jew. When Paul and Barnabas preach about Jesus in the synagogue at Antioch, some welcome his message but some reject it (Acts 13.14–52). To the latter Paul says, 'Lo, we turn to the Gentiles.' 'We turn.' The word 'conversion' is not found in the Bible, but the word that lies behind it, that simple word 'turn', is there on page after page. 'I turn to Christ', I say at my baptism – and I must say the same every day of my life.

Paul himself saw his conversion as a process. Paul knows that he must turn to Christ – and turn again and again to Christ – if he is to be his disciple. That is Paul's 'personal testimony', voiced repeatedly and with unmatched eloquence in his letters. He writes to the Philippians,

> This one thing I do: forgetting those things which are behind and straining forward to what lies ahead, I press on toward the goal for the prize of the heavenly call of God in Christ Jesus. (Philippians 3.13, 14)

Paul's testimony is of someone who knows that he has not got there yet. His testimony is as compelling as it is precisely because it comes from someone who, on his own admission, is deeply flawed. Paul knows that he is fallible; that, like the rest of us, he only 'sees through a glass darkly' (1 Corinthians 13.12). Paul does not always get it right. Some of the things he said about women, for example – 'Adam was not deceived, but the woman was' (1 Timothy 2.14) – appal us. Paul does what he doesn't want to do and doesn't do what he wants to do and, close to despair, bewails his wretchedness (Romans 7.14–25). He wrestles with his 'thorn in the flesh', whatever that was (2 Corinthians 12.7). Paul recognizes that to some of his sophisticated critics the message he preaches is absurd and he, the messenger, contemptible (1 Corinthians 1.18–31; 4.13).

All of which makes the story of Paul's continuing conversion all the more thrilling. The good news Paul preached, that we are saved not by our merits but by the grace of God alone, persuades us as it does because we witness its working in the life of someone who, for all his towering genius, is manifestly of the same stuff as we are.

Joseph of Nazareth

19 MARCH

2 Samuel 7.1–16; Romans 4.13–18; Matthew 1.18–25

LEARNING TO LET GO

Eileen had been trying for some time to sell her house, but with no success. So, responding in some desperation to an advertisement on the web, she ordered a 'St Joseph Statue Home-seller Kit'. The kit, packaged in 'an attractive gift box', duly arrived. It contained a prayer card, a booklet about St Joseph and a five-inch resin statue of the saint, and instructions what to do with it. Complying with the instructions, she immediately buried the statue in her garden. The same day her estate agent was in touch with her with news of a prospective purchaser of her property.

The makers of the resin St Joseph highlight Eileen's story in their publicity for their product. Eileen saw her experience as pointing to 'the amazing power of prayer'. We shall see her story and the tradition it taps into, that it's good to call on Joseph if you want to buy or sell a house, as a further example of the Church's immemorial dilemma about what to make of Mary's husband.

Nothing is known about Joseph beyond the little the Gospels tell us. We learn from both Matthew and Luke of his proud lineage (Matthew 1.1–17; Luke 3.23–38). Beyond that, what we know of Joseph is limited to his part in the events surrounding Jesus's birth and boyhood. The last allusion we have to Joseph in the Gospels is to his occupation as a 'workman' (Matthew 13.55).

Where little is known, legends abound. The wackiest of these is surely the legend that it is on St Joseph's day each year that the swallows return to Capistrano in California. 'When the swallows come back to Capistrano' – the Ink Spots, Glenn Miller, Pat Boone, and Elvis Presley have all recorded their renderings of this tacky old number.

Where legends abound, it is all the more important that we anchor our Christian reflection in what is not legendary. So this St Joseph's day we note that Joseph was 'a righteous man', that he earned his living, and that he learned to let go.

Joseph was 'righteous'. Unfortunately, being righteous does not always tell you what is best. The Jewish law was clear. Joseph and Mary were betrothed but not married. Mary was now expecting a child. Legally Joseph should have set the wheels in motion to establish how Mary had become pregnant (Deuteronomy 22.23–27). But Joseph recognized – dangerous doctrine as it certainly is – that what the letter of the law requires of the righteous is not always the good thing to do. So he decided on a quiet divorce, sparing Mary the disgrace of public proceedings. Justice was tempered with mercy. Joseph acted on the principle, for which his namesake Joseph Fletcher was to argue nearly two thousand years later, that where the law of the land and the law of love conflict you must obey the latter – whatever the consequences (*Situation Ethics,* SCM 1966).

In the light of what the angel told him, Joseph had to think yet again. Neither strict compliance with the law nor defiance of it was the right path. The third way for Joseph was to marry his betrothed. Circumstances alter cases, especially if the circumstances include an intervening angel. We learn from Joseph's story what it means to be righteous in a naughty world. Righteousness is responding in fidelity and obedience to the God of surprises.

Joseph earned his living. Like his maker, he worked with recalcitrant material. We do not know what that material was. That does not matter. Joseph worked and, if we know nothing about his workshop, that only unites him more closely with the mass of humanity. Joseph is one with most who have ever lived whose lives of toil are hidden to history. Whether he welcomes his role as the patron saint of estate agents is another matter. Pope Pius XII, who in 1955 instituted the feast of St Joseph the Worker, said, 'If you wish to be close to Christ, go to Joseph.' 'If you wish to be close to Christ' notice. Not 'if you wish to sell your house'.

Joseph learned to let go. The hardest lesson that every parent has to learn is that our children are not ours. Jesus was not Joseph's, whether or not Joseph was Jesus's biological father. Perhaps Joseph learned to let go sooner than Mary. It is Mary, not Joseph, who reprimands the twelve-year-old Jesus for going off on his own in Jerusalem as the Passover festival concluded (Luke 2.41–51). It is Mary, not Joseph, who still wants to assert her 'ownership' of Jesus at the wedding at Cana (John 2.1–12).

Joseph learned to let go. Perhaps it is for that reason – rather than because he died, so they say, in the arms of Jesus and Mary – that he deserves his title as the patron of a happy death.

George, Martyr, Patron of England

23 APRIL

1 Maccabees 2.59–64 or Revelation 12.7–12; 2 Timothy 2.3–13; John 15.18–21

THERE'S A WAR GOING ON

The pupils of the Archbishop of York's Junior School had a great day out on St George's day 2009. The Archbishop, Dr John Sentamu, invited them to celebrate the day in his garden at Bishopthorpe Palace. Pictures show him surrounded by excited boys and girls. All of them – the Primate and the primary-school children – are waving the flag of St George.

The Archbishop of York, who does nothing by halves, waves the flag of St George with conviction and fervour. He argues that the flag is no longer a banner of bigotry. That, he says, is thanks to the English football team. The national team has made the flag a standard under which the English, of every race and religion, can unite. As he put it in a lecture at the 2009 Oxford Literary Festival, 'Previously an icon of extreme nationalists, a sign of exclusion tinged with racism, the flag of St George instead has become a unifying symbol for a country caught up in the hopes of eleven men kicking a ball around a field.' The Archbishop went on to suggest that perhaps the time is ripe for St George's day to be made a public holiday.

Whether or not St George's day should be a holiday for us all, it already is a Christian festival. Which puts us in a quandary. We all like the idea of another day off, but we are far from sure of what we are doing in honouring George as a saint.

GEORGE, MARTYR, PATRON OF ENGLAND

What do we know about St George? Not much. History is lost in legend. The Pope who canonized him in the fifth century said that his acts are 'known only to God'. The earliest sources say that St George was born in Cappadocia, a region of what today is Turkey. George, the sources say, was a soldier in the army of the emperor Diocletian. Because he spoke up for the Christians in the army, he suffered their fate. He was tortured and on the 23rd of April 303 beheaded. The many legends came later, of which the tale that George slew a loathsome dragon ('half crawling beast, half loathsome bird') to liberate a beautiful princess ('she was as sweet as a summer morning, and as brave as a winter sun') is at once the most famous, the most delightful and the most fanciful.

Our doubts about celebrating St George's day as a Christian festival – whether or not it is turned into a bank holiday – only deepen when we recall what has been done in his name. Muslims remind us of what we prefer to forget, that the Crusaders went into battle under the banner of St George.

How then shall we celebrate St George? The Christian think-tank Ekklesia has mounted a case for a rebranding of the figure of St George. They argue that we should honour George as 'a dissenter against the abuse of power, a contrast to religious crusades, a global figure the English share with other nations, someone who offered hospitality to the vulnerable, and a champion of right rather than might'. For Christians, George is 'a post-Christendom saint'. 'George invites the churches', Ekklesia contends, 'to become better servants of Jesus by abandoning reliance on a romanticized past and, in the case of the Church of England, a legacy of establishment privilege.'

Ekklesia mounts a powerful case. George is the private property of Christians nor of the English. Muslims remember that the Crusaders who ravaged Palestine wore the cross of St George, but at the same time many Palestinian Muslims honour George as a holy man and a worker of miracles. By confronting a Roman emperor on behalf of a victimized minority, and by paying the cost of his courage, George becomes the patron saint of all who pour out their lives for the persecuted.

Such a rebranding of George as a campaigner for just causes is well and good, so long as the old tale of the brave knight, the distressed damsel and the dreadful dragon is not forgotten. That legend may have no roots in history, but it has deep roots in the Christian imagination and in Christian scripture. The tale is a myth, but myths are simply another way – and often the best way – of telling the truth. That is why there are so many of them in the Bible.

Our reading from Revelation is well chosen. It reminds us that the dragon, slaughtered by George, is none other than 'the ancient dragon', whose den is the abyss and whose predatory mission is to deceive and destroy. The myth of George and the dragon is the myth of Michael and the dragon, a myth which makes plain, in a manner no more prosaic account of things ever could, the truth that there is a war going on.

'Like a roaring dragon'– Peter will surely forgive us for tinkering slightly with his text – 'your adversary the devil prowls around looking for someone to devour' (1 Peter 5.8).

Mark the Evangelist

25 APRIL

Proverbs 15.28–33 or Acts 15.35–41; Ephesians 4.7–16; Mark 13.5–13

TO FLEE AND TO FOLLOW

It is a hot night, too hot to sleep indoors. Besides, his mind is racing. The interminable Passover ceremonies he has just sat through have incensed him. Celebrating your deliverance from slavery when you are no freer than you were in Egypt is surely a blasphemous charade. He makes his way up the hillside, turning at last into a small olive grove. The full moon is high, but little of its light reaches beneath the trees where he tries but fails to sleep. Then he realizes he is not alone. He hears the sounds first, the stifled tormented cries. Then he sees him, a man in his early thirties perhaps, collapsed on the ground. Now there are lights beneath the trees and the dancing shadows of men moving up the hill. Some of them are soldiers. He sees them approach the stranger, who has stood up to meet them, as serene and composed as moments ago he was distraught. For a moment, no one moves. Then at once all is confusion. Someone is using a sword. Someone is screaming. Eventually they seize the untroubled figure at the centre of it all. They bind him and take him away.

Something impels the young man to step forward and to follow the prisoner as his guards lead him away through the trees. But then they notice him – and his nerve fails. They reach out to grab him. As they snatch at the linen sheet covering him, he turns and runs away naked.

We are imagining the details, but the incident is on record, on Mark's record (Mark 14.51). The young man who flees naked from Gethsemane is surely Mark himself. Mark makes his fleeting appearance in the story he tells, much as Alfred Hitchcock gives himself a tiny part in each of the films he directs. It is Mark's characteristically cryptic signature on a text which leaves so much unexplained.

Mark turns and runs. Like all the others, he forsook Jesus and fled. This will not be the last time Mark takes flight, though on the next occasion he does so he was, so far as we know, fully dressed. Mark accompanied Paul and Barnabas on the initial stage of their first missionary journey. He stayed with them while they were in Cyprus, but when they set off for Asia Minor he decided to return to Jerusalem (Acts 13.13).

We do not know why Mark dropped out. Perhaps he deplored Paul's methods. Mark will tell in his Gospel how Jesus restored people's sight. Here in Cyprus he has seen Paul strike someone blind (Acts 13.6–12). Maybe Mark felt that something here didn't quite add up. Certainly the miracle made a huge impact, but Mark may have already realized what he will emphasize in his Gospel, that making an impact is not what miracles are for.

Be that as it may, Paul saw Mark's departure as a desertion. When Paul embarked on his next journey, Barnabas wanted to have Mark, who was his cousin, back on board, but Paul refused. Neither of them budged, so they went their separate ways, Barnabas taking Mark with him (Acts 15.36–41). Already missionaries who fall out with each other are carving out their separate territories. Much the same will happen many times in the history of Christian missionary movement.

Mark and Paul do eventually make it up. By the time Paul, now imprisoned, writes his letter to Philemon, Mark is his 'fellow-worker' (Philemon 24). Paul, writing to Timothy, speaks of Mark as someone 'useful to my ministry' (2 Timothy 3.11). The tenor of the comment is not wholly pleasing. I hope that I valued my curates for more than what use they were to me. We are bound to wonder which of the two, Paul or Mark, had to draw more deeply from the wells of Christian forgiveness and forbearance in effecting their reconciliation.

It would be nice to know what Mark thought of Paul, but we don't. It would be nice to know what Mark thought of Peter, another 'deserter', who – so tradition has it – told him all about Jesus, but we don't. What matters is that we know what Mark thought of Jesus. We know what Mark *thought* of Jesus, notice. Although Mark's Gospel was the first to be written, it is as much a theological account of Jesus as the others. That does not mean that Mark explains everything. On the contrary, Mark does much less explaining than do the other Gospel-writers. Mark's reluctance to explain reflects his recognition of the essential mystery of Jesus.

It is Mark who tells us that one day Jesus was walking ahead of his disciples and that 'they were amazed and those who followed were afraid' (Mark 10.32). The Jesus to whom Mark testifies is always ahead of us. We have to do our best to keep up with him. Only in that way will we find out who he is.

Philip and James, Apostles

1 MAY

Isaiah 30.15–21; Ephesians 1.3–10; John 14.1–14

FINDING – AND BEING FOUND

Philip and James have to share the same feast-day. They won't mind. Thanks to the fourth Gospel, we know a little about Philip. About James, we know nothing beyond the fact that he was one of the twelve apostles and that he was the son of one Alphaeus. There are possibly eight individuals named James in the New Testament. A good way to acquire a bad headache is to try to disentangle them and to speculate whether this or that James is to be identified with that or this James. Clearly our James is not to be confused with James, the brother of John and the son of Zebedee. The latter is an altogether bigger fish. He is 'James the Great'. Our James is 'James the Less' – a much more Christian title.

Were it not for John's Gospel, Philip too would be just a name on a list. We meet Philip four times in John. Those four appearances allow us a glimpse of the historical Philip. More important, they illuminate aspects of our own discipleship.

Philip's first appearance is when Jesus 'finds' him. Jesus's first word to Philip is his first and last word to all his disciples – 'Follow me.' Philip then 'finds' Nathanael. The first thing he says to his friend is not, as we might expect, 'Jesus has found me' but 'We have found Jesus' (John 1.43–45). So who finds whom in the story of the call of Philip? John, who delights to say many things at once, leaves us to wonder. 'I sought the one my soul loves' is the song of the bride in the Song of Songs (3.1), but it is the song of the bridegroom too. Our hearts are restless until they find their rest in him, but his heart is restless too until it finds its rest in us. The seventeenth-century Phineas Fletcher found that hard to believe.

Can this poor soul the object be
Of these love-glances, those life-kindling eyes?
What? I the Centre of thy arms' embraces?
Of all thy labour I the prize?
Love never mocks, Truth never lies.
Oh how I quake: Hope fear, fear hope displaces:
I would, but cannot hope: such wondrous love amazes.
('The Divine Lover')

God in Christ finds Philip. In Christ Philip finds God. Such wondrous love amazes.

'We've found him', says Philip to the sceptic Nathanael who, no matter how long ago he was born, is a child of the twenty-first century. Philip's response to his scepticism is not to reason with him but to suggest that he meet Jesus and then make up his own mind. That is the nature of evangelism – not to browbeat by argument but to broker a meeting. It was John the Baptist's method. John said, 'Look at the Lamb of God!' – and then he cleared off (John 1.36).

Philip's second appearance is in the drama of the Feeding of the Five Thousand (John 6.1–14). Philip doubts whether they could ever afford to feed such a crowd – and confronts Jesus with his doubts. That is the right thing to do with doubts.

Philip, who introduced Jesus to Nathanael, is asked to arrange a still more significant meeting. It is his third appearance in John's gospel. Some 'Greeks', we read, want to see Jesus. Their appeal to Philip to fix this meting is the pivot on which John's Gospel turns. 'The Greeks' are the Gentiles. Their plea to see Jesus demonstrates that what the Pharisees have said of Jesus is already being fulfilled: 'the whole world has gone after him' (John 12.19).

Why do the Greeks approach Philip with their request to see Jesus? Presumably they approach Philip because, quite simply, Philip is approachable. John famously observed that 'the Jews have no dealings with the Samaritans' (John 4.9), but nor would they, most of them, have had more dealings than necessary with any others beyond their own number. Philip, it seems, is exceptional. The traditional boundaries do not bother him. He is at ease with those who live in the light of stories other than his own. Philip gets on with Gentiles. And so it is to

Philip that the Gentiles turn with the appeal that Jesus has been waiting to hear, the cry of the world to see him. It is, for Jesus, the signal that his hour has come (John 12.20–23).

'The Jews have no dealings with the Samaritans.' Nor for that matter do many Christians. We default to our own when we have the choice. That is why clergy, although they protest to the contrary, love meetings of clergy. It is safe to say that Philip, to whom the world turned, would have avoided them like the plague.

The Greeks ask to see Jesus. Philip asks – on what is his fourth appearance in John – what he supposes is a different question. 'Show us the Father', he demands. He has yet to learn – as do we – that that is exactly what Jesus is doing all the time.

Matthias the Apostle

14 MAY

Isaiah 22.15–25 or Acts 1.15–26; Acts 1.15–26 or 1 Corinthians 4.1–7; John 15.9–17

CONSENTING TO THE CONTINGENT

'The lot fell upon Matthias.' It did not fall upon 'Joseph called Barsabbas who was also known as Justus' – possibly to his great relief. Such is the seeming arbitrariness of divine choosing. 'The LORD had regard for Abel and his offering, but for Cain and his offering he had no regard' (Genesis 4.4–5). 'Jacob I loved, but Esau I hated' (Malachi 1.2–3; Romans 9.13). So it is with the call of the original twelve. Jesus is walking along the shore of Galilee. He happens to notice Simon and Andrew, casting a net in the lake, and he calls them. Moments later he comes across James and John and they too are invited to fall in with him (Mark 1.16–20). Had Jesus taken a stroll into the countryside instead of along the shore, his first followers might have been farmers rather than fishermen.

By the toss of a denarius, the vacancy in the apostolic body is filled. Luke tells us that the eleven went ahead with their little lottery in the faith that the result would indicate the one God had elected to succeed Judas. Interestingly, Luke stops short of saying in so many words that Matthias was God's preference. He simply tells us that it was Matthias on whom the lot fell. We are not required to believe that God predetermined the result of the draw. Divine omniscience must not be construed so crudely as to suggest that God knows in advance which way up a coin will fall.

The choice was between two names. Much the same choice faces the British Prime Minister of the day when a new diocesan bishop has to be appointed. Two names are submitted to the PM and he or she must decide which name to commend to the monarch as the one to be invited to the vacant see. One suspects that there may have been Prime Ministers who have resorted to a coin of the realm to assist their decision-making.

We flinch to contemplate the sheer arbitrariness of things. Matthias is chosen; Joseph Barsabbas is not. Jane gets cancer; Joan does not. A blizzard means Bob's flight is cancelled and he misses his meeting in New York. 'For the want of a nail, the shoe was lost' – and, one thing having led to another, so too finally was a kingdom lost.

The collect for St Matthias's day invites us to pray that God will preserve his Church from 'false apostles'. No doubt that is a very pious and proper prayer to pray. But the manner of Matthias's election to his apostolate suggests that there is something even more important that we should be praying for. That is the capacity to consent to the contingent. Most that befalls us is merely the consequence of what happens to happen, not the result of moral choices, ours or anyone else's. The gift to accept with serenity all that is random and accidental in the ordering of things is not the most celebrated of Christian virtues – it's not up there with faith, hope and love – but it is a grace to covet.

We know nothing about Matthias beyond Luke's account of how he comes to replace Judas Iscariot. The absence of facts leaves the field to the fantasists. St Clement of Alexandria claimed that Matthias was unusually insistent on 'the necessity of the mortification of the flesh with regard to all its sensual and irregular desires, an important lesson he had received from Christ, and which he practised assiduously on his own flesh'.

Perhaps Matthias did keep his 'sensual and irregular desires' in check, but it was not for that enviable achievement that he was appointed as the twelfth apostle. Matthias is appointed, as Joseph would have been had the lot fallen on him, not because of his personal qualities or skills, but because he had accompanied Jesus throughout his ministry and could testify authoritatively to his resurrection. What are required in apostolic ministry are not primarily those qualifications a bishop looks for in a candidate he is considering for a vacant living. The successful applicant does not have to be a 'team player' or a 'strategic thinker'. He does not need a sense of humour or an enhanced CRB disclosure. What he has to be is a friend of Jesus. What he has to do is to bear witness to him.

And what of the one not chosen? A wholly fanciful apocryphal text, *The Acts of Paul*, claims that 'Barsabbas, Justus the Flatfoot and others' were imprisoned by the emperor Nero. Those – most of us – on whom the lot does not fall to hold high office will be glad to hear about 'Justus the Flatfoot'. We have no way of knowing whether he, or the Barsabbas mentioned, is the same man as the one pipped to the post for twelfth apostle. But we, the incurably flat-footed, who constantly stumble on the slippery paths of Christian discipleship, will want to honour him.

The Visit of the Blessed Virgin Mary to Elizabeth

31 MAY

1 Samuel 2.1–10 or Zephaniah 3.14–18; Romans 12.9–16; Luke 1.39–49 (50–56)

THE GRACE OF VISITING WELL

'Yesterday I visited the bishop.' That is what I say if I am an English speaker. But if I am an American-English speaker I may well say, 'Yesterday I visited *with* the bishop.' Purists whose mother tongue is 'English English' deplore this transatlantic usage. They point out that 'visit' is a transitive verb. It requires an object. You visit a friend, say, or an art-gallery, or – nowadays – a website. Introduce the 'with' and you confuse everybody. 'I visited with the bishop', say the purists, can only mean that the bishop accompanied me on my visit – and I need to go on to say where we went merrily together, the bishop and I, or whom we went to see.

But whether or not the American 'visiting with' is good English, the usage allows a vital distinction to be made. Visiting someone is relational. Visiting a place is not. Pay a call and someone else is always involved, even if the door is slammed in your face. That essential relational aspect of the personal visit is captured by the American idiom. 'Visiting with the bishop' conveys, however clumsily, that the bishop is party to my visit. 'English English' does not distinguish grammatically between visiting the bishop and visiting the bathroom.

On the feast of the Visitation, bad English makes for good theology. So we gladly, if ungrammatically, celebrate the occasion when 'Mary *visited with* Elizabeth'. Elizabeth must be as much in focus as Mary. It is her day too. Popular piety of an earlier age encouraged a wider focus still. A devotional work in extensive circulation in the years before the Reformation was *The Mirror of the Blessed Life of Jesus Christ.* The Franciscan author sees the Visitation as a family occasion. 'Ah, Lord God!' he writes. 'What house was that, what chamber and what bed in which dwelled together so worthy mothers and with so worthy sons, that is to say Mary and Elizabeth, Jesus and John. And also with them dwelling the worshipful old men, Zechariah and Joseph! This was a blessed company of men and women and children.'

Mary 'visits with' Elizabeth and she 'visits with' the unborn John too. It is his day as well as hers. His prophetic ministry has already begun. He is doing what he will be born to do. Unborn babies kick. This one points. That, at least, is the theological subtext of Luke's story. Elizabeth knows what her boy is telling her. 'Look, mother, the Lamb of God!'

The author of *The Mirror* wants us to be sure to leave no one out in visualizing and pondering Mary's 'visit with' Elizabeth. We must not forget either 'the worthy sons' or 'the worshipful old men'. This is much more than a quiet conversation between two women. 'A blessed company' is meeting here. In Elizabeth's exultant exclamation, in John's joyful leaping, above all in Mary's jubilant *Magnificat*, there is an anticipation of heaven.

There is, however, a more down-to-earth moral to the story of the Visitation. It is simply that visiting – in most people's view the supreme virtue of a good vicar – is an excellent thing for all of us to do. When Mary calls on Elizabeth, says *The Mirror*, we have an example of how valuable it is for 'devout men and women to visit each other for edification and ghostly recreation'. To visit is godly. It is what God does. 'In the time of this mortal life' Jesus Christ 'came to visit us in great humility.' Visiting is what Jesus did, both by his incarnation and in his Palestinian ministry.

The grace of visiting well is a gift we are losing in the West. In the rest of the world – I think now of those who were once my African neighbours – visiting is still practised with proper seriousness. In Africa a visit is recognized as a gift that blesses visitor and visited alike.

Because we have forgotten how to visit – we go to dinner parties instead, not at all the same thing – we fail to appreciate much in the Bible that turns on the importance of the giving and receiving of visits and the courtesies that must accompany them. We think of the three men appearing from nowhere at the door of Abraham's tent and how Abraham made haste to make them welcome (Genesis 18.1–8). We recall, by contrast, the perfunctory reception Jesus received in the house of Simon the Pharisee (Luke 7.36–50).

A text towards the end of the Bible touches on the *relational* joy of visiting. 'I have much to write to you, but I do not want to use paper and ink. Instead, I hope to visit you and talk with you face to face, so that our joy may be complete' (2 John 12). '*Our* joy', notice.

We can't be sure who the author of 2 John was. Presumably he was not an American – or he would have said, 'I hope to visit *with* you.'

Barnabas the Apostle

11 JUNE

Job 29.11–16 or Acts 11.19–30; Acts 11.19–30 or Galatians 2.1–10; John 15.12–17

TOUGH GOODNESS

'Barnabas was a good man.' So says Luke. What does that statement tell me about Barnabas? If Luke had told me that Barnabas was a tall man or a fat man I would have known what he meant. Words like 'tall' or 'fat' are adjectives that describe quantifiable characteristics. I can easily tell with a tape measure how high you are or how far it is around your equator. 'Good' is a different sort of word. There is no instrument that will tell me how good you are.

There is no problem when we apply the word 'good' to things. If I say, 'This is a good tooth-pick', all I'm claiming is that this tooth-pick picks teeth efficiently. It is fit for purpose. The problems start when we call people good. Obviously when Luke says that Barnabas is a good man he is saying much more than that Barnabas is efficient.

'Good' is a tricky word. The philosopher G. E. Moore famously said, 'Good is good and that is the end of the matter.' Some say that all you are doing when you call someone good is expressing your approval of them. On this view Luke is doing no more than voicing his admiration of Barnabas – and perhaps implying that we should all be like Barnabas. Luke, we can be sure, would not accept that analysis. Nor should he, because it is a silly notion. Luke certainly approves of Barnabas, but that is because he believes Barnabas *deserves* our approval.

So what was it about Barnabas that led Luke to call him 'a good man'? We have some clues. First, there was the name they gave him. The apostles call him 'the encourager' (Acts 4.36). The word they use is, at root, the term John uses in his Gospel to describe the Holy Spirit as our 'comforter' or 'advocate' (John 14.26). Barnabas then, like God, is one of those who, for all your faults, is ultimately on your side. Sadly, it is a rare quality in Church leaders, some of whom – despite their accomplishments, or because of them – make you want to give up.

Second, Barnabas was not ruled by suspicion and fear. When Saul of Tarsus returned to Jerusalem from Damascus, claiming now to be a disciple of the one whose name he had hated and whose followers he had mercilessly persecuted, Barnabas was the first to reach out to him and to embrace him as a brother in Christ. Barnabas believed that no one is beyond the grace of God.

Third, Barnabas exemplifies the truth that you have to be tough to be good. Joanna Lumley, after whom the Nepalese have named a mountain, would agree. 'Being good is fabulously hard', she says. 'There's nothing wet about being good' (the *Guardian*, 31st August 2009). Barnabas saw that Paul, as he came to be called, could be badly wrong and he had the bottle to tell him so. Barnabas, believing in the wideness of God's mercy, had welcomed Saul, as he then was, as a brother. Barnabas's unwavering belief in the divine mercy led to a showdown. It was all to do with John Mark. Paul had set out on his travels with Barnabas and Mark, but not long into their journey Mark had turned back. Paul saw Mark as a deserter. When Paul and Barnabas started their second missionary journey, Barnabas, convinced that God always gives people a second chance, proposed taking Mark along too. Paul refused the suggestion and, over their disagreement, he and Barnabas parted company (Acts 15.36–41).

There is much about this episode we do not know. But we cannot resist the impression that Paul still had things to learn about Christ's way with people.

It still takes moral courage to insist that on some matters Paul is woefully wrong. Some still bridle if you state the obvious fact that in some respects Paul was a child of his times, merely reflecting the cultural attitudes of first-century society. You still need to be a Barnabas to stand up to Paul. Some might say that had there been more of the ilk of Barnabas across the Christian centuries, women would have been granted their rightful place in the ministry of the Church long ago.

Because of Barnabas, Saul and the apostles exchanged the peace. Barnabas was a reconciler – but he was no smoother. Nice people may be smoothers, but good people never are.

Barnabas is an attractive figure and we would love to know more about him. The late Bishop John Robinson, author of *Honest to God*, believed that we do know more about him. He argued that we have a letter from the hand of Barnabas in the New Testament, the Epistle to the Hebrews (*Redating the New Testament*, London, 1976). It is an appealing idea. One text from Hebrews could be taken as Barnabas's mission statement: 'Pursue peace with every one, and the holiness without which no one will see the Lord' (Hebrews 12.14).

The Birth of John the Baptist

24 JUNE

Isaiah 40.1–11; Acts 13.14b–26 or Galatians 3.23–29; Luke 1.57–66, 80

THE PROPHET CHILD

John the Baptist was a spirited child. 'The child grew and became strong in spirit', we read. The boy Baptist reminds me of my little grandson, Alex. The other day Alex put our kitten in the washing machine. We rescued Bluebell just as the machine was about to start its first cycle.

When Luke tells us that John grew up as a strong child spiritually he is making more than a passing comment. He is saying that, long before he was an adult, John was already fulfilling his role as the forerunner of Jesus. Luke has already told us how the unborn John had pointed to Jesus. We remember John's delight, how he danced up and down in his mother's womb, when Mary, mother of his expected Lord, paid them a visit (Luke 1.39–44).

Now Luke is again linking the one who went ahead with the one who came after. Luke's reference to the growing-up of John anticipates what he will say about the childhood of Jesus. Jesus too was a 'spirited child', a child who grew and became strong as he increased in wisdom and in years (Luke 2.40, 52).

John the Baptist was once a child 'strong in spirit'. That spirited child becomes a spirited adult. John does not jettison his childhood in the way so many of our children do. There are aspects of John's unique ministry that retain the unnerving character of the child. Spirited children are serenely indifferent to what you think about them. At the same time they will say exactly what they think about *you*. The child in John will remain wholly unimpressed by the importance of the grand people – as they supposed they were – whom he met. So 'John the spirited Baptist' will be as outspoken in his denunciation of self-righteous religious dignitaries (Matthew 3.7–10) as he will be in his confrontation with the egregious king Herod Antipas (Mark 6.14–29). And of course he wasn't much worried about what people thought about the way he dressed.

I am also reminded of John the Baptist by my other grandson, who is trotting around our flat as I write. Max, too, is a spirited child. Max is not quite two. Like most children, long before he could say a few words, he could point. He looked – and urged everyone else around to do the same. He still does look, and we pray – for the world is very interesting – that he always will. John the Baptist will one day have many words to say, but all of them add up to one word – that one word: 'Look!' 'Look', he says, 'Look, the Lamb of God' (John 1.29).

All this is to come. On this his birthday we stay with the infant John. The brief account of his circumcision teems with details typical of Luke. Mother, not father, decides what the boy shall be called. (The prominence Luke gives to women in his Gospel suggests that he would not have joined the organization 'Reform' with its insistence on male 'headship'.) There is the typical humorous touch – everyone gesticulating to Zechariah, as if the poor man was deaf as well as dumb. When Zechariah regains his speech they all 'wonder'. Certainly they are 'astonished', as most of our translations put it, but the Greek word Luke uses – and he uses it over and over again – suggests more than mere amazement. Those who 'wonder' are on their way to worship.

If they are lost in wonder, Zechariah is lost in praise. That is how Luke's Gospel has begun and that is how, like all of history, his Gospel will end – in praise. Zechariah sings his *Benedictus*. Our lectionary editors, knowing we are in a hurry, leave it out. This is a pity, not least because it leaves hanging in the air the question with which Luke's little cameo concludes. The hills of Judea are soon ringing with rumours about what's happened. All who hear them 'ponder' these things – literally they 'lay them up in their hearts'. (Yet again, the Authorized Version and the Revised Version are more accurate than the myriad modern versions.) They search their hearts, asking – as we all must in contemplating a newborn child – 'What will this child become?'

Zechariah's song answers their question. 'You, child, will be called the prophet of the Most High.' Is that ascription in some sense true of every child? Does every child 'go before the Lord to prepare his ways'? A woman with a wonderful name thought so and wrote a fine but forgotten book to make her case (*The Prophet Child*, Gwendolen Plunkett Greene, 1927). But those questions are for another time.

Our last glimpse of this spirited child, before he reappears as a hirsute adult chomping on his locusts, is of him 'in the wilderness'. Perhaps one reason why so many spirited children turn into dispiriting grown-ups is because, in these fearful days, they are rarely allowed to experience such places.

Peter the Apostle

29 JUNE

Ezekiel 3.22–27 or Acts 12.1–11; Acts 12.1–11 or 1 Peter 2.19–25; Matthew 16.13–19

FOLLOW MY LEADER

Mark's is the earliest Gospel. The oldest testimonies to its origins claim that behind it stands the figure of Peter. Our earliest source says that Mark was Peter's 'interpreter', whatever that means. Scholarly opinion about Peter's contribution to Mark's Gospel has swung like a pendulum. Most scholars once agreed that Mark gives us Peter's eyewitness account of Jesus. Then there was a scholarly stampede to the opposing viewpoint, with nearly everyone pooh-poohing the early traditions and announcing that Peter had no say whatever in what Mark says. Now the pendulum is swinging back. This about-turn and quick-march back to where we were is largely due to one book – Richard Bauckham's bold, powerful, and persuasive *Jesus and the Eyewitnesses: The Gospels as Eyewitness Testimony* (Eerdmans, 2006).

Title and sub-title provide a digest of Bauckham's book. The Gospels are to be trusted because they rest on what those who accompanied Jesus witnessed. In particular, Mark's testimony to Jesus reflects what Peter saw and heard. If Bauckham is right, then surely our deepest debt to Peter is not so much that he is the bedrock of the Church but that he has enabled us – churchy people or not – to hear the words of Jesus and to see his works.

We do not have to read much of Mark before we meet Peter. Jesus, child of God, 'his spirit yet streaming from the waters of baptism', is walking along the shore of the Sea of Galilee. He sees Peter and his brother Andrew, James and his brother John, and he stops to talk to them. He does not introduce himself. He does not exchange pleasantries. He comes straight to the point. He invites them to play a game. The game, none more serious, is 'Follow my leader'. 'Follow me', he says to them. If, on the feast of St Peter, we do not get much beyond this pivotal event in the human story we shall not have misspent the day (Mark 1.16–20).

The point about the game of 'Follow my leader' is that you must do exactly what your leader does, however preposterous or absurd those actions are. Wherever you are led, there you must follow. 'I have set you an example,' says Jesus, 'that you should do as I have done' (John 13.15). You do what your leader does. He gets crucified; you get crucified. For Peter, Christ's cross will be his. Jesus warned Peter that it must be so (John 21.18). But it is what we all let ourselves in for, if we agree to play this dangerous game (Mark 8.34).

Mark's story starts on the shore of the Sea of Galilee, with the stranger approaching the fishermen. Where the story starts, there the story ends. There is a fearful symmetry to the four Gospels. We come full circle. Mark's is the first of the Gospels, John's is the last. We turn to the closing chapter of John (John 21). 'Jesus revealed himself again to the disciples by the Sea of Tiberias.' The story ends where it began, with the same stranger on the same shore. It ends, as it began, with Peter and the rest being confronted by one unknown.

They do not recognize Jesus. They wonder who he is, just as they did at the start. They wonder all the more when he tells them where to find the fish they'd searched for in vain all night.

Peter leaps into the water. This is not the first time he has acted or spoken on impulse. We think of the Peter who volunteered to walk on the waves to Jesus (Matthew 14.28); of the Peter who, on the Mount of Transfiguration, said the first thing that came into his head (Mark 9.5); of the Peter who boasted that he would never deny Jesus (Mark 14.29). It is interesting to reflect that the first among the first bishops, if that's who Peter was, did not always plan carefully what he said or did in the way that today's bishops insist we all must.

They haul their net ashore, 'full of large fish, a hundred and fifty three of them'. There follows the feast, the breakfast on the beach. Jesus, tacitly forgiving Peter for his three-fold denial, entrusts Peter with the pastoral care of his flock. Then he tells Peter that he will be taken where he will not wish to go. That's the rule of the game, the cost of discipleship. Jesus has one last word for Peter. Peter tries to deflect Jesus's attention to someone else – the way we do – but Jesus is not to be diverted. His last word to Peter is the same as his first – 'Follow me.'

'Follow my leader.' As at the beginning, so now at the close, Peter is invited to play the godliest of games. So it is for each of us, every new day until it's time to put our toys away.

Peter and Paul, Apostles

29 JUNE

Zechariah 4.1–6a, 10b–14 or Acts 12.1–11; Acts 12.1–11 or 2 Timothy 4.6–8, 17–18; Matthew 16.13–19

AN OLD BATTLE AND A NEW NAME

The ruins of Caesarea Philippi are situated on what today are known as the Golan Heights. It is fitting that Jesus's question – none more vexed – 'Who do you say I am?' should have been first asked in one of the most bitterly disputed places on the planet. The Israelis occupy the Heights, but the Syrians insist that they do so illegally, that the land is rightfully theirs. So, across the centuries, rival parties have claimed 'ownership' of Jesus, each staking its claim to be alone entitled to say who he is and how he may be accessed.

Such disputes raged from the start. One of the angriest was between Peter and Paul. Augustine papered over the divisions between them. 'Both apostles share the same feast day,' he said in one of his sermons, 'for these two were one.' In your dreams, Augustine. On the most crucial issue to trouble the early Church – whether or not you had to keep the Jewish law to be a Christian – Paul and Peter had a blazing row (Galatians 1.11–14).

Their row was about power, as all our rows are. Who shall have the last word on matters of doctrine and who shall determine who will and who will not be saved? It is possible that Sunday's Gospel, a passage of scripture as contested as the Golan Heights, reflects just such a dispute within the circles where Matthew's Gospel originally circulated. If so, the text suggests that in those circles it was 'the Peter party', rather than 'the Paul party', that had the best of the argument.

So there may well be echoes in our Gospel of 'battles long ago'. But we need be in no doubt that Jesus did ask his disciples to say who he was and that Peter – the penny from heaven dropping – answered as we are told he did.

Nor need we doubt that Jesus gave Peter his new name. The renaming of Simon Bar-Joseph as 'the rock' is one of the sacred moments of Holy Scripture. To register its significance we must recover some sense – a sense long lost in our frivolous culture – of the sanctity of names. Peter was renamed as, at the last, we all shall be. No greater promise is made to the child of God than that he or she will one day receive 'a white stone in which a new name is written which none knows save the one who receives it' (Revelation 2.17). Commenting on that text, George MacDonald writes, 'The true name is one which expresses the character, the nature, the *meaning* of the person who bears it' (*Unspoken Sermons*, First Series, Alexander Strahan, 1867).

Peter – 'the rock' – is the meaning of the person now so named. Peter's new name was conferred at Caesarea Philippi, yet it was his from the foundation of the world. God's name for someone, says MacDonald, is God's own idea of 'that being whom he had in his thought when he began to make the child'. In the mind of God, Peter was always meant to be what only Peter could be, and meant to do what only Peter could do. So it is for you and me. 'Look to thyself,' says MacDonald, 'for what revelation thou and no one else can give.'

Peter is 'the rock', and on 'the rock' Jesus will establish the alternative society he is already calling into being. Only here and at Matthew 18.18 is that society called 'the church', literally those 'called out'. What – who – exactly is this foundational 'rock'? Is 'the rock' Peter personally, as the play on words would suggest, or is 'the rock' Peter's confession of faith? The arguments either way are nicely balanced. Our interpretation of this text, as of so many others, is likely to be swayed by where we are stabled ecclesiastically. That said, it is obvious that Peter had a leading role among the twelve and in the apostolic church. Peter's grumpy 'I'm going fishing' (John 21.3) would have signalled the end of the Jesus movement for good, had he not left his nets for a second time.

Jesus's alternative society will be ferociously attacked. The gates of the abyss beneath will open and all that is foul and bestial will well up and threaten to engulf it. If that lurid imagery overstates the difficulties we in fact encounter – in paying our contribution to the diocesan common fund, say – then we are possibly not the alternative society that Jesus had in mind.

And what do we make of 'the keys' entrusted here to Peter? From Matthew 18.18 it is clear that he is not the sole custodian of them. The Christian community holds them. Moreover, regardless of whether we ever formally excommunicate anyone, we are unwittingly using the keys given to Peter all the time. If my church is so inhospitable that my neighbour, having turned up the once, never returns, then effectively I have locked the door on him.

Thomas the Apostle

3 JULY

Habakkuk 2.1–4; Ephesians 2.19–22; John 20.24–29

DOUBTING THOMAS – AND DOUBTING JESUS

Thomas doubted but he was far from the first to do so. In the Bible seeds of doubt are sown from the start.

We recall the strange old story. God plants a garden and in it he places a man and some trees. The man is free to eat the fruit of all the trees except one. God tells him that if he eats from 'the tree of the knowledge of good and evil' he will die. God provides a woman to keep the man company. 'At last!' says the man.

Presumably the man and the woman talk to each other – we hope they do – but we are not told what they say to one another. The first conversation we hear is not between the man and the woman, nor between the man and God, but between the woman and a snake. It is the first conversation in the Bible and it opens with an invitation to doubt. 'Did God say?' the serpent asks (Genesis 2, 3.1–7).

'Did God say?' Because we make the same mistake that Milton made in *Paradise Lost* and suppose that the serpent must be Satan, we assume that that was a very wicked thing to ask. We see the snake in the grass as the Devil in disguise and, if it is the Devil who invites us to doubt, then doubt must always be a sin.

But doubt is not a sin. It has been well said that, 'the enemy of faith is not doubt but certainty'. A current of questioning runs through the

Bible from first page to last. Abraham doubts the justice of a God who threatens to destroy the righteous with the wicked (Genesis 18.23–33). Jeremiah accuses God of having deceived him (Jeremiah 20.7). Job, repulsive to his wife, loathsome to his children, abhorred by his friends, rails against the God who, it seems, delights to torture him (Job 19.13–22). It is Job's 'comforters', gathered at his bedside, preaching their sugary certainties, who have no doubts. Doubt is in the bloodstream of the Hebrew Bible, as Robert Davidson shows in his splendid study, *The Courage to Doubt* (SCM Press, 1983).

Thomas doubted, but so do they all. The last we hear of the disciples in Matthew's Gospel is that 'they worshipped yet doubted' (Matthew 28.17). To the two friends, making their sad way home to Emmaus, the rumour of the resurrection is but 'an idle tale' (Luke 24.11). The original ending of Mark's Gospel leaves us, not with the disciples exulting in the certainty of the resurrection, but with the women returning from the tomb in bewilderment and fear (Mark 16.8).

Thomas doubted, but so did Jesus. Jesus doubts whether he can put up with his disciples much longer (Mark 9.19). He wonders whether his own mission will make any lasting impact. 'When the Son of Man comes,' he asks, 'will he find faith on earth?' (Luke 18.8). And, most remarkably, according to the earliest account we have of his death, Jesus's last word is a cry of despair (Mark 15.34).

Thomas had his doubts, but John's Gospel makes it clear that his loyalty to Jesus was not diminished by them. (Thomas is only a name in the other Gospels.) Thomas insisted that he was ready to set off to Judea to die with Jesus, even if as yet he could have had little concept of what 'dying with Jesus' means (John 11.16). Thomas's doubts and uncertainties serve as a spur to his discipleship. It is Thomas who says 'Lord, we do not know where you are going.' It is Thomas who asks, 'How can we know the way?' (John 14.5). We too wonder where Jesus is going. It is for our spiritual well-being that we stay with our doubts about where he is taking us. Those who have no doubts about where Jesus is leading them are the ones more likely to lose touch with him.

Doubting Thomas demands palpable proof of Jesus's resurrection. Jesus invites him to touch him, to probe his wounds. There is no suggestion that he in fact did so. There in the upper room Thomas meets Jesus and it is that encounter that is the basis of his response in trust and worship, rather than any intimate examination of Jesus's resurrection body. Conclusive evidence of the resurrection would not only remove the possibility of doubt. It would also eliminate the possibility of faith.

What songs should we sing for St Thomas? 'One more step along the way I go' by Sydney Carter would be one good choice. Sydney Carter told something of his own story in a book with a wonderful title – *Rock of Doubt* (Continuum, 2005). Carter did not fear his doubts but welcomed them. With our doubts to goad us on there is no risk of our becoming complacent in our faith, of our stagnating in our certainties. 'Trust the truth,' Carter wrote, 'and keep on digging.'

Mary Magdalene

22 JULY

Song of Solomon 3.1–4; 2 Corinthians 5.14–17; John 20.1–2, 11–18

THE SENSUAL, THE SPIRITUAL AND THE NEED TO LET GO

'By night on my bed I sought him whom my soul loves.' Who is she, this lass lying awake and longing for her lover? Who is this lovesick maiden, who searches the streets for her beloved and who, when she finds him, takes him to her never to let him go? The cycle of poems, from which our first reading is taken, does not identify her. Nor do these sublime songs come with a guide to their interpretation. We have some explaining to do.

The songs that make up the Song of Songs – to give the book its proper title – are love poems. They are sometimes boldly erotic in their tone and imagery. Traditionally, they have been interpreted allegorically. Jewish readers have understood the Song of Songs as an allegory of God's love for the children of Israel. Christians have taken the text to be about the relationship of Christ and his Church, or to symbolize the relationship of Christ and the individual believer. St John of the Cross brooded on the Song of Songs in the darkness of his Toledo prison. For him, the maiden who by night is united with the one she loves is the soul who 'by the road of spiritual negation' has attained union with God. The Song of Songs, on this view, has nothing to do with sex. It is all to do with 'the dark night of the soul'.

Most modern commentators dismiss these allegorical interpretations. Some see the fact that in the Middle Ages the Song of Songs was extraordinarily popular with monks and nuns – they copied this text more than any other – as evidence of how screwed-up those vowed to chastity become. We are urged today to enjoy the Song for what it is, a celebration of physical love. The implication is that we are now at last free from the inhibitions that led earlier generations of Bible readers to spiritualize the Song of Songs. Because we are now mature enough, sufficiently at ease with our sexuality, we can enjoy the text for what it clearly is, a rhapsody in praise of the joy of sex.

In response to such facile observations, the comment of the American scholar Judith Ernst is worth quoting. 'To suddenly "discover" that the Song of Songs is a secular erotic text, and to strip it of centuries of mystical and allegorical significance, is to express an arrogance that is uniquely modern' (*Song of Songs*, Eerdmans, 2003).

The Song of Songs is a sacred text. It is not a raunchy book which somehow found its way into the Bible because no one noticed what it was really about. All our loves – *eros* as well as *agape* – can be paths to God. The Song of Songs, while never mentioning God by name, has a spiritual dimension that transcends the text's eroticism. But the spiritual does not expel the sensual. Rather it intensifies it. Certainly the flesh may sometimes be stronger than the spirit, but flesh and spirit are not enemies. Passion can pass into prayer. Dante loved Beatrice no less when his love of her was caught up in his love of God.

We are instructed to read this deeply erotic, deeply spiritual text on the feast day of Mary Magdalene. We know very little about her. She is named as one of the women whom Jesus had healed and who remained in his company, providing for him 'out of their resources'. Her condition before she met Jesus must have been exceptionally serious. In Luke's graphic language, 'seven demons had gone out of her' (Luke 8.1–3). The women who accompany Jesus – Mary Magdalene is again named among them – witness Jesus's crucifixion 'from a distance' (Mark 15.40–41). According to John's Gospel, she is the first to witness the risen Jesus, although she does not immediately recognize him. There are no further references to her in the New Testament.

Mary Magdalene is widely supposed to have made a living out of the kind of carnal loving the Song of Songs delights in. It would be unfortunate if, by reading from the Song of Songs on her special day, we tacitly lent support to this supposition, for it is groundless. There is no reason to identify Mary Magdalene with the unnamed woman of doubtful reputation who anoints Jesus in the house of Simon the Pharisee (Luke 7.36–50). Needless to say, there is no substance either in the piffle put about concerning her in recent pulp fiction and on ten thousand barmy websites.

There is one connection, however, that we are meant to make. The unnamed maiden of the Song of Songs holds her lover and refuses to let him go. Mary too wants to hold on to Jesus, to have the reassurance of his continuing presence. But to her, as to us, such reassurance, such certainty, is denied. Mary must 'take leave of Jesus'. Whether or not we must in the same way take leave of God, we must certainly jettison our idolatrous ideas about him.

James the Apostle

6 AUGUST

Jeremiah 45.1–5 or Acts 11.27–12.2; Acts 11.27–12.2 or 2 Corinthians 4.7–15; Matthew 20.20–28

CLIMBING LADDERS AND STEPPING DOWN

I recently met a friend of a friend who has made it his ambition to become a member of the General Synod of the Church of England. He is putting himself about. He is making sure he is noticed. He is prepared to do all it takes to be elected to Synod, even if it means attending innumerable tedious meetings of lesser consequence. My friend's friend is not motivated by self-aggrandisement. He is driven by a genuine longing that the Church of England should bear better witness to the Christian gospel. He believes that the changes needed to make the church more effective can be brought about only if those of his evangelical persuasion use the democratic processes by which the church is governed to secure a majority in Synod. My friend's friend wants power – but only so he can make a difference.

Ambition is not always so selfless. When James and John, the sons of Zebedee, ask for the highest places in Jesus's coming Kingdom – a realm not to be confused with the Church of England, or even its General Synod – they do so because they want to be more important than everyone else (Mark 10.35–45). Their appetite is not to serve, but to be served. They want people to look up to them. Their quest for power is not because powerful people can make things better, but because powerful people are adulated. (In Matthew's account, the appointed Gospel for St James's day, it is the pushy mother who demands a place at the top table at the Messianic banquet for her boys. By focusing on the mother rather than the sons, Matthew wants to avoid presenting the disciples in an unfavourable light. But James, like his brother, was a 'Son of Thunder' (Mark 3.17). (Someone with that nickname was surely no mother's boy.)

James of course had already had a glimpse of glory. He was there on the mountain where Jesus was transfigured (Mark 9.2), just as – with John and Peter – he witnessed the raising of Jairus's daughter (Mark 5.37–43). But James must learn that the road to glory goes through Golgotha. That is why Jesus keeps James near to him, again with John and Peter, in the garden of Gethsemane (Mark 14.33).

Even after that lesson, even after the cross, did James still hanker after prominence? Perhaps he was consciously and conspicuously carving out a position of leadership for himself in the church in Jerusalem. Perhaps that is why Herod Agrippa I, puppet-king of Judea, had him put to the sword. Be that as it may, this 'Son of Thunder' was the first of the twelve apostles to be martyred.

Today James, or what remains of him, receives the veneration he craved. In 813 a bishop in the north-west of Spain made a timely discovery. He found some bones in a cave and announced that they were those of James. The bones were put to good use. The beleaguered Spanish were fighting a losing battle against the Muslim armies. St James's intercession in heaven and his intervention on earth were invoked. The tide of war turned. St James became *Santiago Matamoros*, 'St James the Moor-slayer' – an ascription missing the Christian point, though no more so than does the title 'St James the Great'.

Today those purported relics of St James rest in the crypt of the cathedral of Santiago de Compostela. Pilgrims come in their tens of thousands to pray at his shrine, some crossing half of Europe on foot to do so. Their pilgrim's path is known as *El Camino de Santiago*, 'The Way of St James'. On his feast day we who seek a city more beautiful than Santiago de Compostela ask what the Way of St James is for us.

That way is not the way of *Santiago Matamoros* ('Herod decapitated me; I'll decapitate you'). It is rather the way of Jesus made plain in the Gospels, the narrow way leading to life. The way of St James is the way of the cross. The world offers other paths. Those are forbidden to us by the word of Jesus, 'It will not be so among you.'

'It will not be so among you', says Jesus. But, alas, it *is* so among us. Forging a career, for example, entails forcing ourselves past those falling behind. Our quiet pleasure in being noticed, however well-concealed behind a mask of self-deprecation, becomes addictive. We sought high office so that we could do some good and then we noticed one day that we were relishing our position more for its perks and its purchasing power.

A good topic for a Bible study on St James's day would be the place of ambition in the Christian life. Such a meeting might have a word of advice for my friend's friend who so badly wants to be on General Synod.

The Transfiguration of Our Lord

6 AUGUST

Daniel 7.9–10, 13–14; 2 Peter 1.6–19; Luke 9.28b–36

WORSHIP BEYOND WORDS

Our lectionary rightly sends us to Luke. His account of the Transfiguration is much the same as that of Mark and Matthew, but it has touches of his own which draw us more deeply into the mystery of what took place. Only John probes the mystery more profoundly. For John the whole ministry of Jesus was a manifestation of divine glory in transfigured human flesh.

Luke, and only Luke, tells us that Jesus ascended the mountain *to pray*. Luke is inviting us to see what unfolded on the mountain as an act of worship. He wants us to understand that the ultimate purpose of worship is to share in glory, the glory which is creation's goal. Luke, with Matthew and Mark, relates that Moses and Elijah appear with Jesus. But it is only Luke who adds that they too appear 'in glory'. Their work accomplished, they too are transfigured. Transfiguration, Luke implies, is not just for Jesus. It is our destiny too. The transfiguration of our dust is our Christian hope. Our present affliction, St Paul writes, is preparing us for 'an eternal weight of glory beyond measure' (2 Corinthians 4.17).

That final transfiguration does not mean the loss of individual identity. Moses and Elijah are 'in glory', but they are still Moses and Elijah. They can carry on a conversation. They are talking with Jesus about his imminent 'exodus', a word which does indeed mean departure, as it is usually translated, but which means so much more – as Moses for one well knew.

Peter, James and John saw Jesus as, one day, every eye shall see him. They 'saw his glory'. Peter felt he had to say something. He offers to pitch three tents on the mountain top, one for Jesus and one each for the two radiant figures accompanying him. Kind commentators, being nice to Peter, suggest that he was talking sensibly. Peter is insisting, they suggest, that some kind of accommodation must be provided for the glory that has been manifested, just as the divine glory was housed in the tabernacle in the wilderness. Luke realizes that Peter is simply wittering. As he laconically comments, 'he did not know what he said'. As if glory can be bottled or put up for the night.

If Peter was the first clergyman – a suggestion no more absurd than the claim that he was the first Pope – then it is not surprising that he felt obliged to say a few words. The compulsion to speak, even when it would clearly be better not to, is powerful in some people. It's in their genes. Many made this way are drawn to professions where they can talk to their heart's content. They become schoolteachers, say, or members of parliament. Or they get ordained.

But never being at a loss for words is not an asset in a Christian minister. When we speak of God our words invariably mislead. If we experience God, the saints testify, our words utterly fail. On the feast of St Nicholas in 1273, in a church in Naples, the Dominican Friar Thomas Aquinas said Mass as usual before beginning a day of lecturing and writing. During the Mass, something happened to him. He experienced an overpowering mystical vision. Afterwards, he ceased writing his great *Summa Theologiae*. 'All that I have written', he said, 'appears to be so much straw after the things that have been revealed to me.'

In the end garrulous Peter shuts up – if only for a time. Luke adds a final comment, a detail that Matthew and Mark do not mention and one that we too, alas, often overlook. Luke's last word is of the first importance. 'They kept silent and in those days told no one of any of the things they had seen.' What took place on the mount of Transfiguration was an experience of worship beyond words.

But if nothing can be said about such an experience, there is everything to be done about it. The word of God from the cloud, the symbol of glory, is 'This is my Son, my chosen; *listen to him*!' 'Listening' in the language of the Bible always means obeying. At the summit of the mountain the disciples witness the glory of God in the face of Jesus Christ. At the foot of the mountain, they are confronted by a disabled child. They are not required to speak of what words cannot describe. A more practical testimony is demanded.

A Quaker with a glorious name, Ben Pink Dandelion, has written, 'Our testimony is what we do from our experience of God, not what we say. Testimony is not creed, but action' (*Celebrating the Quaker Way*, Quaker Books, 2009). It is what we might call 'the transfiguration cycle', the cycle of worship, silence – and then getting on with what must be done. It is a cycle, not a sequence, for we usually find that what we do is not much good. Then we must go back and wait on God.

The Blessed Virgin Mary

15 AUGUST

Isaiah 61.10–11 or Revelation 11.19—12.6; Galatians 4.4–7; Luke 1.46–55

MARY'S MAGNIFICAT AND OURS

Every evening we sing Mary's song. Whatever do we suppose we are doing, making her words ours? The *Magnificat* is an intensely personal statement. It is the testimony of a young woman who has been told that she will become a mother while still a virgin. Moreover, she learns that the child she will bear will be the Son of God. Mary's song wells from her heart, but it also arises from a situation which is, to say the least, unusual. Her circumstances are unlikely to be experienced by any of us who join in the *Magnificat* for the umpteenth time. So what on earth am *I* doing when *I* say, 'Behold from henceforth all generations will call me blessed'?

I make Mary's *Magnificat* my own, because I need to make her mind my own. I need to grasp what she makes of what is happening to her. To be sure, Mary's role in universal salvation is unique. (Excepting always the possibility – 'every star shall sing a carol' – that in worlds beyond our own many another Mary bears a saving child.) Mary's destiny is hers alone, but what Mary sees in her story is the way God always works. Mary recognizes in her experience, unparalleled as it is, the pattern of how God deals with any of us. He is a God who 'looks with favour on lowliness'. I sing along with Mary so that I may take that truth to heart.

That principle, that God works with and through the lowly, those who make no claims for themselves, the empty-handed and downhearted, informs the whole of Mary's song. Mary sees how God has dealt with her personally as the manner of his activity throughout history. Just as God has exalted her, the lowliest among women, so God, working across the generations and among the nations, has lifted up those of no account, and brought low the proud and powerful.

Mary's tenses are past tenses. For her, the reversal of the old order has already taken place. Is this wishful thinking – leading to what perhaps we might call 'wishful singing'? She sings her song of the scattering of the proud, but the Romans still rule her land. The crucified bodies of those who dared challenge Roman authority hang from their crosses along the roads Mary walks. But we need not suppose that she closed her eyes to this reality. The case is rather that Mary believes so confidently in the outcome of the mission of her son that she can speak and sing of God's purposes through him as already accomplished.

Have we the faith, two millennia later, to do the same? Dare we sing Mary's song of the overthrow of the powerful in a world where warlords terrorize, where the corrupt in government siphon into their Swiss bank accounts the aid intended for their impoverished people, where dictators rule over the starving and where we all are at the mercy of international financiers?

We rarely ask ourselves to consider those questions as we stand to sing Hymn 186 in *The New English Hymnal*. Timothy Dudley-Smith's rousing rendering of the *Magnificat*, 'Tell out, my soul, the greatness of the Lord', is indeed a fine hymn. But although it changes the past tenses of Luke's text to present tenses, it still requires us to assert untruths – unless, that is, we bring to our singing the faith that Mary brought to hers and insist that we are affirming the certainty of what, in Christ, is bound to be.

'Powers and dominions lay their glory by!' No, they do not. 'Proud hearts and stubborn wills are put to flight!' No, they are not. 'The hungry (are) fed, the humble lifted high.' As I write, in 2010, the hungry are still hungry and the humble still humiliated. We can sing the *Magnificat* with conviction only if we can sing it with Mary's conviction, with the faith that, however long it takes, this is how one day it will be. 'Hail Mary, full of grace, pray for us . . .' As we honour the Blessed Virgin Mary, we plead for her to pray that we may be delivered from 'triumphalism', from the religious euphoria that floats far adrift from the truth of how things actually are.

The Australian Catholic Social Justice Council has published a prayer based on the *Magnificat*. The sober tone of this bold new text is evident in its first line: 'My soul comes in darkness and unknowing, seeking understanding of the happenings of these days.' This antipodean *Magnificat* recognizes the realities of Mary's relationship with her son. Certainly she holds to her faith that God has 'looked with favour on her lowliness'. Her 'let it be' (Luke 1.38) is unwavering. But there is much about Jesus that, like the rest of us, she does not understand (Luke 2.50).

On Mary's day, we turn to her – and with her turn to her Lord and ours – 'in darkness and unknowing'.

Bartholomew the Apostle

24 AUGUST

Isaiah 43.8–13 or Acts 5.12–16; Acts 5.12–16 or 1 Corinthians 4.9–15; Luke 22.24–30

HIDDEN SERVICE

Bartholomew is said to have been flayed alive before being crucified upside down. Leather-workers look to him as their patron saint. In painting and sculpture he is often represented as holding a knife, with his own skin neatly draped over his arm. Quite how such imagery is supposed to deepen our devotion is unclear.

As with other obscure figures among the twelve, in the absence of factual the Church has embraced the far-fetched. The fantasies about Bartholomew abound – that he went on a missionary tour to India, that Emma, the wife of King Canute, entrusted one of the apostle's arms to Canterbury Cathedral, that he can be efficaciously invoked if one suffers from nervous tics. But although Bartholomew has given his name to famous hospitals, such as 'Barts' in London, there is no evidence that he was any more adept than the other apostles at the healing miracles attributed to all of them.

We know nothing about Bartholomew. There is even some uncertainty about his name. It has been suggested that Bartholomew and Nathanael were the same person. All we know about Bartholomew is the only thing that matters about him. We know that he was a disciple of Jesus. That's all. Bartholomew himself would not have wished anything else to be told about him.

In thinking about Bartholomew, about whom nothing is known apart from his fidelity to Jesus, we are made aware that the call to serve can be a call to *hide*. What attracted Thomas Merton to the monastic life, especially to the Trappist life, was its promise of total *hiddenness*. 'The thought of those monasteries,' he writes, 'those cells, those cloisters, those men in their cowls, the poor monks, the men who had become nothing, shattered my heart' (*Seven-storey Mountain*, Harcourt Books, 1948). For Merton, it is only because of these 'Bartholomews', men so hidden as to be absent from the earth, that God is persuaded to stay his hand a little longer before bringing our tragic tale to a close.

Today's Job Centres do not advertise vacancies for 'servants'. The term is felt to be shameful and demeaning. Servants, we suppose, belong to a Victorian upstairs–downstairs world. Servants languished in the station in life into which they were born, by day in the scullery, by night in the attic. In the age and culture of the 'service industry', where billions are made overnight, the very notion of service has become corrupted.

Jesus has made the role we have come to despise for all time his own. 'I am among you', he says, 'as one who serves.' The saying, one of the great 'I am's' of the Gospels, is only in Luke, but it is uttered in the accents of John. Here is one of the moments in Luke's Gospel where 'the beloved physician' and 'the beloved disciple' speak as one. When we hear these words, we are in heart and mind where John takes us, in the upper room where Jesus rose from the table to wash his disciples' feet (John 13.1–20).

The disciples notice what Jesus does only because he has assumed the role of someone normally unnoticed. The household slave goes about his work and, for the rest of the house, it is as if he does not exist. Popes and vicars who conspicuously wash people's feet once a year have missed the point.

To serve is to hide. He who comes from 'the God who hides himself' (Isaiah 45.15) hides himself too. On Easter Day, on the road to Emmaus, Jesus met two disconsolate disciples. Later, after he had made himself known to them, 'he vanished from their sight' (Luke 24.31). That is what Jesus does. He still vanishes from our sight. Now you see him; now you don't. He does not await our recognition, still less our ovations. By the time we have found the noisy hymn to sing his praise, he is off somewhere else.

We know, many of us, that we have met him. There was that moment, at the edge of an abyss, when he touched our lives, steadied us, and saved us from falling. Only later did we recognize who it was – and by then he had gone. He had moved on, as he did in Galilee. And as in Galilee, we must drop everything and follow him.

There are the Bartholomews whose hidden service to their sisters and brothers only becomes known when they have left us, when they themselves are lost in light. There are many more Bartholomews whose story – before the books are opened – we shall never know.

George Eliot was no believer, but in the famous closing words of the greatest novel in our language, she honours Bartholomew.

For the growing good of the world is partly dependent on unhistoric acts; and that things are not so ill with you and me as they might have been, is half owing to the number who lived faithfully a hidden life, and rest in unvisited tombs.
(*Middlemarch*)

Holy Cross Day

14 SEPTEMBER

Numbers 21.4–9; 1 Corinthians 1.18–24 or Philippians 2.6–11; John 3.13–17

GET REAL – TOUCH WOOD

The Church of the Holy Sepulchre in Jerusalem houses two of Christendom's most holy sites and exhibits several of its most horrendous schisms. The uniquely hideous edicule, beneath the main dome of the building, is claimed to cover the tomb from which Christ rose. Custody of this structure is shared between the Greek Orthodox, the Roman Catholic and the Armenian Apostolic churches. The Copts have a minuscule altar round the back.

The site of the cross – through the main doors, turn right, and up the stairs – is in the custody of the Orthodox. The feast of the Holy Cross – the Orthodox call it 'the Exaltation of the Holy Cross' – commemorates the finding of 'the true cross' in this place by Helena, mother of the emperor Constantine, and the dedication of the original church at a two-day festival held on the 13th and 14th of September, 335.

The Greeks guard the site jealousy. A few years ago on this feast day, someone left the door open to the adjacent Catholic chapel and the Orthodox took this as an insult. A fist-fight broke out which had to be broken up by the police. 'See how these Christians love one another.'

Devotion to the cross as the instrument of our salvation is common to every tradition of Christian piety. The Orthodox and the Catholics have their reliquaries and the Protestants have their hymns. The same instinct to contemplate the wood where our Saviour hung inspires both pilgrimages to the Chapel of the Holy Relics in the Santa Croce church in

Rome and the hearty singing of 'When I survey the wondrous cross' at the Keswick Convention. That instinct is not unchristian. It is incarnational. Stuff matters. Things are good. Spiritualism is more of a foe of Christianity than materialism. Only when they are put to wrong use do things go bad. Never was timber better used than on Good Friday. High and low alike, we all sing from the same hymn-sheet. We all 'cling to the old rugged cross' and, until we 'exchange it some day for a crown', we shall go on doing so.

We sometimes speak of the cross, on which Jesus died, as a tree. 'Calvary's tree', we call it. It is a powerful image. We fell by the fruit of a tree, so says the strange old story. In the Garden of Eden we reached out and helped ourselves to the forbidden fruit, the fruit of the tree of the knowledge of good and evil. And it stuck in our throat.

We fell by a tree. But we are also saved by a tree – the tree on Golgotha, on whose dead branches Jesus Christ was impaled. And then, at the last, so we are told, we shall be made whole by a tree. The Bible closes with the tremendous vision of the garden-city of God where, by the banks of a bright river, there grows a tree – the tree, says St John, 'whose leaves are for the healing of the nations' (Revelation 22.2). The tree in the garden, the tree in the Roman killing field, and the tree in the holy city, the New Jerusalem – the three trees are one.

According to tradition, the cross was made with wood from the tree from which the apple was taken. 'Out of that very tree that made us suffer, began our salvation after it had carried him who was both God and man.' So the tree that was our scaffold, our gallows, becomes our only hope. A medieval poet hears the cross speak: 'I beheld the healer's tree till I heard how it broke silence, best of wood, and began to speak. "Lo, the Prince of Glory, heaven's Lord, hath glorified me above all forest trees."'

In the Church of the Holy Sepulchre you are shown where the tree that was in that first garden stood. It is immediately beneath the site of the cross. 'We think that Paradise and Calvary, Christ's cross and Adam's, stood in one place.' So said the poet, so say the guide books, so says our Christian intuition.

Archbishop Rowan Williams knows about the cross. He's been there. Some would say that's where we put him. While he was still Primate of Wales, Rowan Williams preached at a service at the start of a meeting in Hong Kong of the Anglican Consultative Committee. It happened to be Holy Cross Day. Here is a snippet from the Archbishop's sermon:

> All I want to say about the image of the Holy Cross this morning is that the Cross of our Lord Jesus Christ is where we wake up. 'Awake

sleeper and rise from the dead and Christ will give you life.' Our sin is like sleep, like a bad dream. We are locked in ourselves. The serious tangled insides of the human mind, the human heart, human speech trap us more and more. Here the reality of God stands against the reality of our minds and hearts.

Get real. Touch wood.

Matthew, Apostle and Evangelist

21 SEPTEMBER

Proverbs 3.13–18; 2 Corinthians 4.1–6; Matthew 9.9–13

IT TAKES ALL SORTS TO MAKE A CHURCH

'Follow me', says Jesus, and at once Matthew walks out of his office, without even stopping to switch off his computer. At the same word of command, and with no more idea of what he was letting himself in for, Peter had earlier left his nets to join Jesus (Matthew 4.18–22).

Matthew was a 'publican'. Publicans were cogs in the wheels of empire. They were locally employed functionaries, contracted by the Roman authorities to oversee public works and to fill many of the countless pen-pushing posts needed to keep the vast imperial machine ticking over.

Tax-collecting was farmed out to publicans. They bid for the right to collect the taxes due from a given area. They paid upfront what was owed. Then they recouped their outlay by raking back the cash from the local people. Any profit was their own. Manifestly the system was open to abuse. Our Gospel-writers lump tax-collectors together with 'sinners' in general. For the people of the first-century Roman Empire, any tax-collector you met was bound to be on the make.

Matthew had a desk job. The Gospel specifically tells us that he was 'sitting' when Jesus called him. Peter, the fisherman, didn't sit very often and probably had a healthy contempt for those who did. Those who are up and about at their work usually dislike those who earn their living sitting down, especially when the latters' living is at their expense. It must have rankled with Peter that he should have had to toil all night to maintain the likes of Matthew in the comfortable lifestyle to which he had become accustomed.

It is a mischievous thought, but we might wonder whether this first-century dislike of publicans has something in common with a characteristically twenty-first-century antipathy. Perhaps they felt about Matthew what we feel today about managers. Teachers, on their feet all day in front of classrooms of disaffected teenagers, resent being told what to do by sedentary mandarins who would not survive for five minutes in their situation. Nurses and doctors are angry at the extent to which their working lives are now controlled by apparatchiks who could not tell the difference between a bedpan and a defibrillator. Clergy, too, are being managed as never before, not always, so far as they can see, to the glory of God and the furtherance of his Kingdom.

Whether or not Matthew was himself profiteering from tax-collecting, he was tarred with the same brush as those who were. It could not have been easy for Peter and the other fishermen to have accepted Matthew as a fellow-disciple, especially if Matthew had been the tax-officer they previously had had to deal with professionally.

But Peter has to accept Matthew. The hardened fisherman, with no time to sit down, must embrace as his brother the flabby taxman who, until Jesus came his way, rarely stirred from his cushions. The fastidious civil-servant must fall in step with the one who still whiffs of fish. It takes all sorts to make a church.

Not that Jesus objects to Matthew's cushions. Jesus reclines on them – that's what the Greek word means – when he has a meal at Matthew's house. The parallel account in Mark's Gospel, where Matthew appears under the name of Levi, makes it clear that that is where they all eat together (Mark 2.13–17).

The lurking clergy protest. They 'speak out', as clergy are supposed to. They object to Jesus's consorting with Matthew and other disreputable characters. 'Those who are well have no need of a physician,' says Jesus, 'but those who are sick.' The wonderful irony of this reply escapes them. Jesus has his own views about who are ill and who are healthy.

The irony does not escape us. That of course does not mean that we are in any better health than those whom the irony passed by.

Matthew left his desk to follow Jesus. Did he one day return to his desk and sit down again to write the story of Jesus which now bears his name? It is most unlikely. The Gospel itself is anonymous. The traditional ascription to Matthew is tacked on later. 'Matthew's Gospel' is clearly reliant on earlier accounts of the words and deeds of Jesus, notably on that credited to Mark.

This does not mean that we could manage without the Gospel we call Matthew's. Matthew's story – whoever the Matthew the evangelist was –

is *his* story of Jesus, providing a perspective on Jesus that is his own. Above all, for this Gospel-writer, the story of Jesus is an 'old, old, story'. Hence the Old Testament texts with which his Gospel teems. One text seems to have been especially dear to our 'Matthew', for he quotes it twice. As we hear on Sunday, Jesus tells his carping critics, 'Go and learn what this means: "I desire mercy, not sacrifice" ' (Hosea 6.6).

He has said the same before (Matthew 12.7). He wants us to get the message.

Michael and All Angels

29 SEPTEMBER

Genesis 28.10–17 or Revelation 12.7–12; Hebrews 1.5–14 or Revelation 12.7–12; John 1.47–51

ANGELS IN PECKHAM – AND ELSEWHERE

Angels are back. Or rather they have been rediscovered, for of course they have never gone away. Howard Worsley is a scholar who has studied them. He concludes that 'angels appear to be alive and well in ordinary life' (*Through the Eyes of a Child*, Church House Publishing, 2009).

When William Blake was eight years old, he saw 'a tree filled with angels, bright angelic wings bespangling every bough like stars'. Children see angels more often than grown-ups do. That may be because children, their fantasies immune to facts, see what is not there. On the other hand, it may be because, as Jesus said, there are realities, hidden to clouded adult eyes, which are revealed to children (Matthew 11.25).

It was in Peckham in 1797 that William Blake saw his tree full of angels. The twenty-first-century question is whether angels are still to be seen in Peckham. Certainly there are lots of angels in Peckham, if you use the word to describe lovely people. One such is Camila Batmanghelidjh, who founded the children's charity Kids Company and who won the United Kingdom's Woman of the Year award in 2006. She has become known as 'the Angel of Peckham'.

But what of angels as all the Abrahamic faiths speak of them, supernatural beings of supernal beauty, more real than mere mortals? Do you come across them in Peckham? Those offering 'angel healing' would claim that angels are around in Peckham as everywhere else. You can call on them – or pay a fee to be put in touch with them – any time you have a bad back.

Our Michaelmas readings, and all that is said about angels in Holy Scripture, teach me that angels are not at my beck and call, even if my back is giving me gyp. Angels do God's bidding, not mine. God gives his angels different things to do, but their primary task is twofold. They are messengers and guardians. Cherubim, most exalted of angels, guard the way to the Tree of Life (Genesis 3.24). (John Milton sends shivers down one's spine with his description of them, 'with dreadful faces thronged and fiery arms'.) Abraham reassures his steward, when sending him off to find a wife for Isaac, with the promise, 'God will send his angel before you' (Genesis 24.7). The devil knows what angels do. Famously, he reminds Jesus of the Psalmist's words, 'God will give his angels charge of you' (Matthew 4.6; Psalm 91.11). Most memorably, Jesus warns us never to despise children because angels are their guardians (Matthew 18.10).

In their capacity as messengers, angels move between heaven and earth on the ladder that Jacob – and Jesus too – envisioned as set up between there and here. Strictly speaking, only angels and Jesus use this ladder. It's not something the rest of us can do. But in these matters we should not speak strictly, still less sing strictly. So we happily join in the jolly song, 'We are climbing Jacob's ladder, soldiers of the cross'. So too, rather more thoughtfully and to Stainer's setting, we sing, 'Hallelujah to Jesus, who died on the tree, and hath raised up a ladder of mercy for me'.

Because the role of angels is to bear messages between heaven and earth, it is not surprising that they feature prominently in the story of one who forsook the former for the latter. An unnamed angel appears to Joseph (Matthew 2.20), Gabriel himself appears to Mary (Luke 1.26), and the sky above the shepherd's field is bright with angels. Day by long day, we are invited to rest beside the weary road to hear them sing.

Still through the cloven skies they come
With peaceful wings unfurled.

That is the faith we pray to be rekindled at Michaelmas. Angels are still to be met in Peckham. If Peckham is inconvenient, you can meet them somewhere more central.

Not where the wheeling systems darken,
And our benumbed conceiving soars! –
The drift of pinions, would we hearken,
Beats at our own clay-shuttered doors.

The angels keep their ancient places –
Turn but a stone and start a wing!
'Tis ye, 'tis your estrangèd faces,
That miss the many-splendoured thing.

But (when so sad thou canst not sadder)
Cry – and upon thy so sore loss
Shall shine the traffic of Jacob's ladder
Pitched betwixt Heaven and Charing Cross.
(Francis Thompson, 'The Kingdom of God')

And what of Michael? In scripture he is both disputatious and combative. He has a spat with the devil over the body of Moses (Jude 1.9), a quarrel we need not be drawn into. He overcomes the angelic hosts of the Persians (Daniel 10.12–14, 21; 12.1–3). As we hear in our tremendous text from Revelation, he goes to war in the Last Battle, triumphing over 'the dragon and his angels'. (Not all angels, we notice, are benign.)

There is, however, a gentler side to Michael. Early Christians turned to George for support in battle, but it was to Michael that they entrusted their sick.

Luke the Evangelist

18 OCTOBER

Isaiah 35.3–6 or Acts 16.6–12a; 2 Timothy 4.5–17; Luke 10.1–9

THE LOYAL STAY LOYAL

With the aid of a torch, the physician peered up the child's nostril. 'Good God!' he exclaimed.

I was that child, a little boy having difficulty breathing through his nose. It is my only memory of the man. No doubt technically he was a skilled surgeon for, thanks to the operation he performed, I no longer wander the world with my mouth wide open. But he did not inspire love in me – only terror.

Much can be said about Luke, the medical man, but nothing more telling than that he was loved. For Paul, Luke was simply 'the beloved physician' (Colossians 4.14). Paul loved him and so did everyone else. Why was Luke so loved? Even if we knew far more about him than we do, it would be as difficult to answer that question as it is to explain why – among equally admirable people of our acquaintance – we warm to some and not to others.

We do, however, have one clue to Luke's character. It is in a comment Paul makes in his farewell letter to his fellow-worker Timothy. Paul's valedictory is deeply moving. The apostle is 'on the point of being sacrificed', as he puts it. His end is near. He holds his head high, but his heart is lonely, for many who were close to him have gone. 'Only Luke is with me', he tells us.

The comment underlines Paul's sense of abandonment, but it also says a lot about Luke. Luke was loyal. He was Paul's loyal companion on long stretches of the latter's missionary journeys. Perhaps Luke's loyalty was tested. Others, it seems, found Paul trying. Mark parted company with Paul and so did Barnabas when Paul refused to have him back (Acts 13.13; 15.36–41). Demas deserted Paul (2 Timothy 4.10). But Luke is with him to the end. The loyal stay loyal. We think of Lear's 'all-licensed fool', enduring with him 'the winds and persecutions of the skies', or of Sam, unswervingly faithful to Frodo, even when the malign power of the Ring he bears begins to poison his master's mind.

A remarkable fragment of a poem by Edgar Alan Poe survives:

The pulse beats ten and intermits;
God nerve the soul that ne'er forgets
In calm or storm, by night or day,
Its steady toil, its loyalty.

The fragment is entitled, 'The Beloved Physician'.

Luke's legacy to us is his account of the mission of Jesus of Nazareth and of the emergence of the movement that, to this day, claims Jesus to be 'both Lord and Christ' (Acts 2.36). The Gospel that bears his name and its sequel, the Acts of the Apostles, together take up more than a quarter of the text of the New Testament. We can be grateful that one who wrote so much wrote so well. Luke is the supreme story-teller of the Christian Bible. He understands that the Christian faith is the story of someone who invites a personal response, not a series of assertions demanding assent.

George Caird, a fine New Testament scholar, went as far as to say that Luke 'was more interested in people than ideas' (G.B. Caird, *Saint Luke*, Penguin Books, 1963). We can see why he said this. The people who we meet in Luke and only in Luke are unforgettable – the good

Samaritan (Luke 10.25–37), the wastrel son and the waiting father (Luke 15.11–32), the woman who anoints Jesus's feet and wipes them with her hair (Luke 7.36–50), and many more. But Caird's comment misses a vital point, not only about Luke's narrative style, but also about the Christian gospel. The truth of God is incarnate in Jesus, not in the Nicene Creed, say, or Calvin's *Institutes*. So it is in Luke's Gospel. Luke's 'ideas' – and he has many of them – are not lifeless abstractions distilled from the cavalcade of events and people. What Luke believes – above all, that God's love is for all humanity, embracing 'the last, the least, and the lost' – is embodied belief.

Luke's story does not pass into propositions, but into prayer and worship. His account of Jesus ends with the disciples returning to Jerusalem where 'they were continually in the temple blessing God' (Luke 24.53). They do not stay there, of course. Their journey will take them from Jerusalem to the ends of the earth (Acts 1.8). Like Luke, they too will be storytellers, telling the tale of someone to be trusted rather than prescribing tenets to be subscribed to.

We have joined them on that journey. We shall meet many people on our way. What shall we tell them? Luke might suggest that we take to heart the words of Philip Pullman – not someone usually seen as an ally of the Christian cause.

> You must tell them true stories, and everything will be well, everything. Just tell them stories.
> (*The Amber Spyglass*, Scholastic, 2000)

Simon and Jude, Apostles

28 OCTOBER

Isaiah 28.14–16; Ephesians 2.19–22; John 15.17–27

SAINTS NOT CELEBRITIES

The Church does not celebrate celebrities. It celebrates saints. The distinction is an important one. The lives of celebrities are public exhibitions. The notion of a hidden celebrity is a nonsense. It is otherwise with the saints. We may know a lot about some saints, but about most we know little or nothing. And none of that great company – not Simon, not Jude – would have it otherwise. We honour them for their very hiddenness.

For Luke, Simon was 'Simon the Zealot' (Luke 6.15, Acts 1.13). For Matthew and Mark he was 'Simon the Cananaean', a translation of the Hebrew *qana*, 'the zealous one' (Matthew 10.4, Mark 3.18). Both titles amount to the same and to much less than is sometimes made of them. To describe Simon as a 'zealot' does not necessarily mean that he belonged to one of the terrorist groups committed to the violent overthrow of the Romans. (Still less likely is the legend that he was crucified in the market town of Caistor, Lincolnshire, on the A46 to Cleethorpes.) That he was called 'the zealot' simply means that he was zealous. Was it perhaps a teasing and ironical nickname for the one of the twelve who in fact was the most relaxed and laid-back?

Jude is 'Jude the equally obscure'. He is, literally, 'Judas of James' (Luke 6.16, Acts 1.13), that is to say, 'Judas, the son of James'. Presumably he is to be identified with the mysterious 'Thaddaeus' who appears in the lists of the apostles in Matthew and Mark (Matthew 10.3, Mark 3.18). A little letter with a lovely ending ('Now unto him who is able to keep us from falling . . .'), which just makes it into the New Testament, is attributed to Jude 'brother of James'. But all we really know about Jude is who he wasn't. He was 'Judas not Iscariot' (John 14.22). It is our Jude, not Judas Iscariot, who asks why it should be that Jesus reveals himself to some and not to others. Behind that question there can, of course, lurk a less innocent complaint, 'Why don't others see things my way?'

Because his name continued to recall his unfortunate namesake, there was initially a resistance to invoking Jude. So he became 'the saint of last resort'. Eventually 'the saint of last resort' becomes 'the patron saint of lost causes' (including, we learn, the Chicago Police Department), and in that capacity countless desperate people still turn to him. Their prayers and their thanks to him are posted in the press and on the web. Sue pleads to St Jude, 'Please help me. I am unemployed, alone and becoming depressed about my situation. I need a job ASAP and please heal my cat's ears.'

In the absence of historical evidence, speculation and superstition flourish. Neither, incidentally, is to be despised. Aversion to speculation can merely be atrophied imagination. The piety, however naïve, that begs Jude to heal Tibbles is truer to the spirit of Christian prayer than the scepticism that can only voice devout generalities.

And so I pray, 'Most holy apostle, St Jude Thaddeus, faithful servant and friend of Jesus, the name of the traitor has caused you to be forgotten by many. But the Church honours and invokes you universally as the patron of hopeless cases, of things almost despaired of. Pray for me, I am so helpless and alone.'

Our Gospel addresses a community feeling helpless and alone. In John's language, the Church is suffering the hatred of 'the world'. We picture the Christian gospel spreading like wild-fire around the Mediterranean. But there must have been many occasions when the Kingdom of God appeared as forlorn a cause as any taken to St Jude. The repeated warnings in the Gospels that towards the end hard times would come reflect situations where those hard times were already being experienced. In the imagery of the New Testament, the last battle has already begun. The Jesus of John's Gospel encourages a beleaguered Church to see its afflictions as the wounds of the war that will truly end all wars, the divine engagement with sin, suffering and death, the final outcome of which is certain.

Meanwhile we have some Christian common sense from our Old Testament reading. The New Revised Standard Version's 'One who trusts will not panic' captures the force of the text that the older and more literal versions memorably translate as, 'He that believeth shall not make haste.' Sometimes a Kierkegaardian dread overwhelms us, a 'sickness unto death', and we wonder how much of a lifetime has been spent in pursuit of lost causes – such, perhaps, as disentangling the different lists of the apostles in the New Testament.

One commanding more authority than Corporal Jones tells us not to panic. The cause of the Kingdom is not lost, but it is not best served by headless chickens.

Andrew the Apostle

30 NOVEMBER

Isaiah 52.7–10; Romans 10.12–18; Matthew 4.18–22

APOSTOLIC NETWORKING

In Matthew, Mark and Luke, Andrew is little more than a name. He is wholly overshadowed by his brother Simon Peter. (Was Andrew the younger of the two, we wonder; even as an adult still the small boy who can never quite keep up with his big brother?) John, however, introduces us to Andrew as an individual in his own right. With all due deference to our appointed Gospel, on the day Andrew has to himself, it is to John's account of him we turn.

John's Andrew is good at 'networking' (He is, after all, a fisherman.) Networkers put people in touch with people. John noted Andrew doing this three times, on each occasion to great effect.

Andrew was a disciple of John the Baptist. Like John, he was longing for the one who was to come. Andrew, when we first meet him, is simply standing there with John, together with another of the latter's disciples. Then Jesus appears, as he had the previous day, almost out of nowhere – except that John has told us, in his Gospel's tremendous prologue, that, far from coming from nowhere, Jesus comes from God.

John the Baptist, we hear, 'looked at Jesus as he walked' – which, incidentally, is what we are all doing whenever we read the Gospels. John tells his two disciples to do the same. He bids them see Jesus. The writer of the Fourth Gospel chooses his words for their weight-bearing capacity. To 'see' Jesus in his Gospel is to recognize him for who he is.

What follows is highly dramatic, although the account of it is sparing. Andrew and his companion hear John's words and, we read, 'they followed Jesus'. 'They followed Jesus.' That's all. So momentous an event, so tersely told – as if all that happened was that two people wandered off with someone else. But for the Gospel-writer, their abandonment of John for Jesus marks the end of the old order and the beginning of the new. It is the first day of what Paul will call 'a new creation' (2 Corinthians 5.17).

Now Andrew 'networks'. He 'finds' his brother Simon and tells him that he has 'found' the Messiah. Again John chooses little words to carry great weight. Andrew brings his brother to Jesus and then, it seems, slips away. Such is Christian mission. All it is is drawing attention to someone else (John 1.35–42).

Andrew does the same the next time we meet him. We are on the shore of the Sea of Galilee. A huge crowd has followed Jesus, hungry to see his works. Now their hunger is more basic, for they need something to eat. Only Andrew notices the child. 'There is a little boy here', he says. (Almost all our modern versions miss the diminutive.) We must dwell on these words. Andrew does not suppose that the boy's picnic will be any use. But at least he notices the child and he invites Jesus to notice him too. In the event the child's snack becomes a feast for the multitude. Everyone tells us that 'the feeding of the five thousand' is all about Holy Communion. Presumably the child himself shared in the feast which – with some assistance from Jesus – his gift provided. Curiously, the Christian Church, at least in the West, will later insist that children go hungry at the very meal this miracle symbolizes (John 6.1–14).

Andrew appears for a third and final time in the Fourth Gospel. Once more he is networking. Already he has put his brother Simon in touch with Jesus. Already he has put a child in touch with him. Now, with his fellow-disciple Philip, Andrew puts Gentiles in touch with Jesus. These 'Greeks', as John calls them, tell Philip that they wish to see Jesus. Philip tells Andrew and together they tell Jesus. That is how networking works.

It is a moment of critical importance in John's story of Jesus. It is the moment Jesus has long awaited, when the world beyond his own people turns to him. For Jesus, the Gentiles' request to see him – with all that 'seeing' in this Gospel means – is the sign that his 'hour' has come, the hour when, in and beyond his death, he will be 'glorified', the hour when the grain of wheat must die and so bear fruit (John 12.20–24).

Andrew then passes from our story. He is listed with the other apostles in Acts (Acts 1.18). The rest is silence. (The fanciful legends, the X-shaped cross and so on, need not detain us.)

It could be said that, unlike his brother Peter, Andrew doesn't actually do very much. He merely puts people in touch. Yet Andrew's networking has eternally important consequences. He tells his brother about Jesus. He draws attention to the child. He tells Jesus that the Gentiles too are seeking him. All that he does diverts attention from himself. That is not always how those in the apostolic ministry behave.

Stephen, Deacon, First Martyr

26 DECEMBER

2 Chronicles 24.20–22 or Acts 7.51–60; Acts 7.51–60 or Galatians 2.16b–20; Matthew 10.17–22

DEATH OF A DEACON

In celebrating the festivals that follow nose-to-tail after Christmas, we draw on dwindling reserves. We have had too much to eat. The house is in a mess. The overexcited children are getting fractious. If we are ministers of religion, we have spent far too much time in church. We are exhausted and we need a break. Such are this season's 'sordid particulars', as T. S. Eliot calls them. Nevertheless, in them, he says, 'even now the eternal design may appear' (*Murder in the Cathedral*). The principle, that the purpose of God is worked out in the tiresome actualities of how things are, is shown by the testimony of all the saints, starting after Christmas with Stephen, John and the Holy Innocents.

The 'sordid particular' which led to the appearance of Stephen in the Christian story was a bitter row in the congregation. (There is nothing new under the sun.) In 'the church' in Jerusalem there were daily hand-outs to the destitute, particularly for the widows, always a desperately needy group in antiquity. ('The church' was of course not yet a separate organization, but simply a movement within Judaism which looked to Jesus of Nazareth as Messiah.) The dispute was between 'the Hebrews' and 'the Hellenists'. The Hebrews were the Jews of Jerusalem and Judea. The Hellenists were from Jewish communities from around the Roman world. The row was about whether this relief programme was being administered fairly. Tensions between Brits and Poles and disputes over entitlement to social services come to mind. The apostles declined to be involved in the messy business of manning soup kitchens. They pleaded that they had sermons to prepare and prayers to say. So they appointed Stephen and six others to run the church's relief programme.

But Stephen does not confine himself to the humble tasks of a 'deacon', if that's what he was. He turns out to be something of a radical and a firebrand. He is brought to trial before the Sanhedrin, accused of blasphemy. His speech in his own defence concludes with a searing attack on his accusers. By murdering Jesus they have proved themselves to be no better than their predecessors who persecuted the prophets. But what seems to have most outraged the hierarchy, what sealed his fate and brought a rain of rocks down on him, was that he dared to challenge the institution of the temple itself (Acts 6, 7).

Stephen is the first martyr – or 'witness'. By forgiving his executioners, he bears eloquent witness to his Lord who did the same. But the story of Stephen shows too that from the start Christians have fallen out with one another. There was the spat over the daily hand-outs, certainly, but reading between the lines there were clearly far deeper differences of opinion among those first Christians. Their fundamental disagreement was over the importance of structures such as temples, over 'houses made with hands'. In a word, they disagreed over whether or not Christianity requires religion.

Persecution breaks out on Stephen's death, but we are told that it does not touch the apostles (Acts 8.1). That is unsurprising. After all, so far from attacking the temple, the apostles have been turning up there religiously – *religiously* – every day (Acts 2.46). Then as now in the Church, there seem to have been the traditionalists and the liberals. The apostles erred on the side of caution, as to this day those who think of themselves as their successors usually do. Such are the 'sordid particulars' of the body of Christ on earth. Thus it was in the beginning, is now, and – until the Lord comes again – ever shall be.

Stephen, like Jesus, is dragged out of the city to die and, like Jesus, he dies forgiving his killers. Watching how he dies, we ask ourselves what forgiveness means and costs, if forgiveness is to be more than a facile form of words. We watch *how* Stephen dies, but we ponder too the implications of *why* he died. For not only did Stephen die in the same manner as Jesus did; he died for the same reason that Jesus did.

Jesus was crucified for sedition, because Pilate was persuaded that he posed a political threat. But it wasn't for political reasons that those who sought the death of Jesus wanted him out of the way. Sedition was simply the charge they came up with, because it was the one accusation Pilate had to take seriously. The real reason they wanted to be rid of him was because they recognized that he was a threat to the religious structures they held dear, especially the temple.

The first nail in Christ's cross was hammered in on the day that Jesus, in a blazing outburst of the wrath of God, launched his assault on the temple and, on that same day, the first rock was hurled at Stephen.

John, Apostle and Evangelist

27 DECEMBER

Exodus 33.7–11a; 1 John 1; John 21.19b–25

THE WORD BECAME OUR AGEING FLESH

A story is told of the last sermon preached by John, the beloved disciple. He was the pastor of a little church in Ephesus. He was by now a frail old man, the last disciple alive who had seen and heard and touched Jesus in his days on earth. His congregation knew that that Sunday would be his last. When it came to the sermon, the elders of the church supported their beloved pastor and set him in a chair before his people. John gathered what little strength remained to him, drew what would be almost his final breath, and whispered his last words to them: 'Little children, love one another. It is the Lord's command and it is enough.'

'Love, as I have loved.' It is, as John discerns, the distinctive ethic of Jesus. It is a compass, not a map. It is not a sat-nav on your dashboard, telling you exactly when to turn left or right. It does not give instant answers to vexed questions. The command to love as Jesus loved points the direction. It is 'true north'.

John has his own term for the sphere of 'the sordid particulars' in which even now 'the eternal design may appear'. It is the sphere of 'the flesh', that troublesome and variously hued substance, much pampered and indulged at Christmas, which the Word became in his incarnation (John 1.14).

We need to be specific. Whose flesh did Christ make his in order that 'the eternal design' might appear? When we say that our Lord took his human nature from his blessed mother we speak truly. But that statement does not exhaust the implications of John's audacious claim. We must press the question. Whose flesh exactly is his? Who is John talking about when he says that the Word became our flesh? Suicide bombers? Homophobic bishops? Drug-dealers? A salutary discipline would be to write down the names of those individuals who happen to get up our nose – and then to add by each name, 'The Word became *his* flesh' or 'The Word became *her* flesh'. Then each of us would need to add to that list their own name. My unlovely flesh, John tells me, he made his.

John will have marvelled that the Word became his flesh. If he lived as long as they say he did he will have marvelled all the more, as all of us must as the years pass. For it is not only young firm flesh he makes his; old flaccid flesh too, blotched, puckered and shapeless, he makes his own.

Robert Browning's poem 'A Death in the Desert' is a study of how John's testimony to the Incarnation is informed by his experience of the Word become his own failing flesh, flesh 'that hath so little time to stay'. The veil of the beloved disciple's flesh is now so thin that he is nearly 'bare to the universal prick of light'. Those devotedly attending him wonder whether, if they chafe his hands, he might yet speak. At first John only smiles – 'smiles and loves and will not be disturbed'. Then a boy fetches a tablet in which a text is engraved. He presses the apostle's fingers on 'the deeper dints' of the text and now John breaks his silence. He reads the imprinted words, 'I am the Resurrection and the Life.' Then John speaks of his Gospel, his written witness to the

Word made flesh. He explains how he was given to see clearly and steadily truths that previously had been only glimpsed:

> What first were guessed as points, I now knew stars
> And named them in the gospel I have writ.

There follows – and it is the bulk of the poem – a long last discourse from St John. John wants the grieving circle around him to understand that, until the veil of the flesh finally falls away and 'law, life, joy, impulse are one thing', we can never be sure that we know fully. Yes, what he 'guessed as points, he now knew stars', but even to know that much is still – as Paul has it – to know only in part (1 Corinthians 13.12). Man must accept that:

> What he considers that he knows today
> Come but tomorrow, he will find misknown.

John's Gospel concludes with an ironical editorial footnote. The irony is so light and oblique that it is rarely noticed. The editors assure us that they know John has told us the truth in his Gospel, but they add that Jesus did much more than is recorded in its pages (John 21.24, 25).

This last comment is more than a mildly interesting aside. We have only a very small part of the story of Jesus. It follows that, while what we say about him may or may not be heretical, it is certainly more or less mistaken, as we shall discover when dawn breaks.

Meanwhile: 'Little children, love one another. It is the Lord's command and it is enough.'

The Holy Innocents

28 DECEMBER

Jeremiah 31.15–17; 1 Corinthians 1.26–29; Matthew 2.13–18

CHILDREN ON THE CROSS

The day before yesterday we honoured Stephen as a 'deacon' and a 'martyr'. Yesterday, we gave thanks for John, 'apostle' and an 'evangelist'.

We have some understanding of what these terms mean, but what, please, is a 'holy innocent'? We have enveloped the infant victims of Herod in so much incense that we can no longer see them. Do we suppose that the tiny tots skewered by Herod's soldiers were holier or more innocent, whatever those words mean, than the kids up the road who escaped the carnage?

Here are the first children we meet in the story of Jesus and already we sense the hesitancy and equivocation about the status of children that has always beclouded Christian thinking about them and that continues to bemire its ministry to them. Hard heads soften. Augustine witters. These little ones, he says, are 'buds, killed by the frost of persecution the moment they showed themselves'. One steadier voice speaks, that of Pope Leo the Great (400–61):

> They were able to die for him whom they could not yet confess. Thus Christ, so that no period of his life should be without miracle, silently exercised the power of the Word before the use of speech . . . Christ crowned infants with a new glory, and consecrated the first days of these little ones by his own beginnings, in order to teach us that no member of the human race is incapable of the divine mystery, since even this age was capable of the glory of martyrdom.
> ('Sermon on the Solemnity of the Epiphany')

Not that there was anything particularly glorious in the 'sordid particulars' of being butchered by one of those soldiers. But we take Pope Leo's point. Bethlehem's slaughtered children are martyrs, a title and status that has nothing to do with their 'innocence' or 'holiness', still less with any precocious piety we suppose they displayed. Theirs is the 'graced vulnerability' that both makes them helpless before Herod and sets little children at the centre of the Christian church (*Graced Vulnerability*, David H. Jensen, Pilgrim Press, 2005).

We used to say, before the law was belatedly changed, that those old enough to die for their country should be allowed the vote. By the same token, those old enough to die for Christ – even if not yet three – should surely be allowed the sacrament of his love for them.

Matthew understands the massacre of Bethlehem's children as answering to Jeremiah's haunting description of Rachel weeping inconsolably for her children, slaughtered when Jerusalem fell to the Babylonians. Matthew's method is to take Old Testament texts and to make up stories which can then be interpreted as their fulfilment, as if those texts were predictions of what would happen centuries later. So we have the stories of the Journey of the Magi (Matthew 2.1–11) and of the Flight into Egypt (Matthew 2.13–15). But Matthew must not be supposed to be misleading us by such a method of story-telling. If we are misled, it is not by Matthew but by our mistaken assumption that what a story teaches depends on whether it happened.

In truth, the story of what Herod did to Bethlehem's under-threes is anchored in history. Whether or not Herod indiscriminately murdered all Bethlehem's under-threes in the hope of thereby eliminating the threat posed by one child in particular – and he was butcher enough to have done so – what he allegedly did is what countless tyrants certainly have done. The voice of Rachel, weeping for her children, is heard throughout history.

At the Festival of the Holy Innocents we contemplate the suffering of children. We think of children who are victims of cruelty or neglect. We think of children who suffer lingering painful illness. We think of children dying of hunger. We think of children caught up in natural disasters.

Because it is too easy to think in such generalities, we hold in mind – if we dare – the single image. So I think of a nameless newborn baby girl, dumped in a Delhi station toilet, discarded simply because she's female. I think of Pintu working in a tannery, surrounded by piles of stinking cattle flesh, and not paid a penny – a twenty-first century slave. I think of the Jewish baby, impaled on a Nazi bayonet. I think of the Haitian child, surviving for days under the rubble of his fallen home in Port-au-Prince until he finally succumbs to his thirst.

Each such child is the child on the cross. The Feast of the Holy Innocents and Good Friday are the same day. The spear of Herod's soldier and the Nazi bayonet are both thrust into Christ's side. The whimpering unheard cry from the child beneath the rubble – 'I'm thirsty' – is the dying word of Jesus.

And so we pray,

Lord, give to men who are old and tougher,
The things that little children suffer
(John Masefield, *The Everlasting Mercy*)

CELEBRATIONS

Thanksgiving for Holy Communion (Corpus Christi)

Genesis 14.18–20; 1 Corinthians 11.23–26; John 6.51–58

AN ACT OF DEFIANCE

I shall never forget a simple service of the breaking of bread which a small group of us shared in a hotel bedroom in Kiev in what was then the Soviet Union. This was long before the collapse of communism. At that time what we were doing was illegal. In that atheist state religious observances were only permitted in registered churches, those churches which were prepared – quite literally – to toe the party line. Had we been caught celebrating our unlawful Eucharist, we would have been put on the next flight home. Had we been local Christians discovered doing the same thing, we might have found ourselves spending years in an unpleasant place in Siberia.

Recalling that clandestine celebration, I think of the most moving words ever written about the Mass. Dom Gregory Dix's monumental study of the Eucharist, *The Shape of the Liturgy*, was published on the Festival of Corpus Christi 1943. Towards the end of this great work, Dix's measured prose suddenly takes flight. In a soaring passage of surpassing power he offers his own thanksgiving for the countless different ways in which Christians have heeded Christ's words, 'Do this in remembrance of me':

> Was ever another command so obeyed? For century after century, spreading slowly to every continent and country and among every race on earth, this action has been done, in every conceivable human circumstance, for every conceivable human need from infancy and before it to extreme old age and after it, from pinnacles of earthly greatness to the refuge of fugitives in the caves and dens of the earth . . .

Towards the end of this sublime passage, too long to quote in full, there are the words which seize me as I remember that little service held behind locked doors in a hotel room behind the Iron Curtain. Dix is rehearsing the myriad ways in which Christians have obeyed Christ's command:

> tremulously, by an old monk on the fiftieth anniversary of his vows; furtively by an exiled bishop who had hewn timber all day in a prison camp near Murmansk; gorgeously for the canonization of St Joan of Arc . . .

'Furtively by an exiled bishop who had hewn timber all day in a prison camp near Murmansk . . .' Why do we give thanks for Holy Communion? We do so for many reasons and to list them is to risk intoning all too familiar pieties. Here, moved by the memory of the Mass we offered secretly in Kiev, moved too by the thought of the sacrifice offered – for once the words must carry their full weight – by a bishop in Murmansk, I dwell on another reason for giving thanks for Holy Communion. What we do is always *an act of defiance*.

Holy Communion is rooted historically and theologically in the celebration of Passover. Passover begins when a child asks, 'Why is this night different from other nights?' The Eucharist too is different, defiantly different. It is a defiant enactment of an alternative way of doing things, the counter-cultural way of life which Jesus described as 'the reign of God'. Those who break bread in memory of Jesus affirm what in every age the world has denied, that 'we who are many are one body'. The Eucharist creates, if only for an hour on a Sunday morning, a society ruled by love rather than power. By partaking of 'one bread', we defy the devil to divide and conquer us.

Paul writes, 'There is no longer Jew or Greek, there is no longer slave or free, there is no longer male and female, for all of you are one in Christ' (Galatians 3.28). Every Eucharist refutes the cynical assumption that it can never really be like that.

Sadly, what we assert at the Holy Table it often contradicted by how we are and what we do. Paul's words to Galatians would need to be rephrased if addressed to us, with whom there is still Jew and Greek, still slave and free, still male and female – and, we might add, still child and adult – for we are not yet one in Christ.

It is essential that we pay attention to the context in which Paul describes 'the institution of the Lord's Supper'. If we take that account out of context, as our lectionary does, we draw its sting. Paul mentions the Lord's Supper only because he wishes to highlight the scandalous infighting that was going on in the church at Corinth. Such conduct was making a mockery of the meal. Such conduct still does.

What we affirm in liturgy must be exemplified in life.

Lord Jesus Christ,
we thank you that in this wonderful sacrament
you have given us the memorial of you passion:
grant us so to reverence the sacred mysteries
of your body and blood
that we may know within ourselves
and show forth in our lives
the fruits of your redemption.

Dedication Festival

YEAR A

1 Kings 8.22–30 or Revelation 21.9–14; Hebrews 12.18–24; Matthew 21.12–16

YEAR B

Genesis 28.11–18 or Revelation 21.9–14; 1 Peter 2.1–10; John 10.2–29

YEAR C

1 Chronicles 29.6–19; Ephesians 2.19–22; John 2.13–22

John Inge, Bishop of Worcester, has written a fascinating book about the importance of place (*A Christian Theology of Place*, Ashgate, 2003). In the bishop's view, we are losing our sense of place and that loss dehumanizes us. Bishop Inge believes, as everyone once recognized, that place matters and places matter.

In the past, place was always important to people of faith. There were places where, as all knew, the veil between this world and another was thin, where the transcendent was experienced, where you went to meet your God. Such places were called 'holy'. We still refer to 'holy places' – many are mentioned, for example, in tourist guides to the so-called 'Holy Land'. But while pilgrimages to so-called holy places do continue, our awareness, at least in the West, of place and of the holiness of places is much diminished. We are seriously dislocated.

The Bible has mixed views about holy places. Some holy places are heinous places. The Israelites are instructed to destroy all 'the high places' of the Canaanites. Their failure to do so is repeatedly condemned in the Hebrew Bible. Bad kings build high places to false Gods and even good kings fail to tear them down (1 Kings 13.33; 22.43).

Ambivalence about holy places is most apparent in the conflicting attitudes to the temple we find in the Bible. Any simple points we make at a Dedication Festival about the temple are likely to be simplistic. In building the temple, Solomon was carrying out the project his father David had in mind and for which he had secured divine planning permission. Solomon's temple was a sumptuous edifice. The fact that it was built by slave labour does not bother the Biblical writers.

Nor does it trouble them that the temple was designed like a pagan shrine, with its outer courts, inner courts and innermost sanctuary for the deity ('the most holy place'). That ground plan is replicated in 'the tabernacle', where we are told the Israelites worshipped in their wilderness wanderings. (We owe our account of the tabernacle to the nostalgia and imagination of priestly writers, writing long after the destruction of the temple.) Solomon's pagan architecture is, alas, repeated in thousands of Christian churches, with their chancels, screens and sanctuaries, cordoning off the areas of the building reserved for especially holy people like clergymen.

The problem about the temple and about all holy places is that God cannot be supposed to be in one place more than another. Solomon prays, 'Even heaven and the highest heaven cannot contain you, much less this house that I have built.' So it is that, while prayers are to be said 'towards this place', it is from 'heaven his dwelling place' that God will answer.

This distinction proves to be too subtle by half. The temple itself comes to be seen as 'God's house' and becomes an object of veneration. The prophets take opposing sides. Some condemn this devotion to the temple as idolatrous (Jeremiah 7.4). Others continue to see the temple as the pledge of God's commitment to his people and, after its destruction, they demand that it be rebuilt. An angry and petulant God complains, through Haggai, that without his temple he has nowhere to live (Haggai 1).

At a Dedication Festival, we may well hear again how Jesus 'cleansed the Temple'. The point will probably be made that Jesus saw the temple as a house of prayer and objected to its improper us. The simple inference will be drawn that we must look after our churches and make sure that we make the best use of them. They are to be seen – in the kind of infelicitous jargon Jesus never used – as a 'valuable resource'. Again, the simple thought, however edifying, is simplistic.

Was the cleansing of the temple an affirmation of holy places dedicated to the worship of God? The Gospel-writers see it that way and tell it that way. Or was it – what Jesus actually did – an attack, not on the abuse of the temple, but on what the temple itself stood for? Was this Jesus's dramatic announcement that the rites of institutionalized religion are no longer the way to God?

Divided opinion about holy places persists. After Jesus's resurrection and ascension the disciples are 'continually in the temple' (Luke 24.50). Presumably they approve of the place and what goes on there. But before long Stephen is accused of launching a fierce attack on the temple – and what he says in his defence is hardly a denial of the charge (Acts 6.8—8.1).

We are still divided about the significance and role – not to speak of the affordability – of our holy places. A Dedication Festival is the occasion, not to avoid this nettle but to seize it. We shall insist, with Bishop Inge, on the importance of what he calls 'the relationship between people, place, and God'. But we shall want to ask too whether the time has not come to find an upper room somewhere and start again.

Bible Sunday

YEAR A

Nehemiah 8.1–4a (5–6), 8–12; Colossians 3.12–17; Matthew 24.30–35

THE LASTING WORD

One of the many Bibles in my study has an introduction entitled 'How to read the Bible with understanding'. There I read that 'Much of the Bible is not easy to understand and not all is equally rewarding for all purposes.' Few would disagree with this understatement, though some would add that many of our difficulties with the Bible confront us in the very places where its meaning is plain.

Skim the pages of the Bible and you stumble on many texts that are both perfectly clear and deeply baffling.

> 'As one was felling a log, his axe-head fell into the water . . . Elisha cut off a stick and threw it in and made the iron float' (2 Kings 6.1–7).
>
> 'Your nose is like a tower of Lebanon overlooking Damascus' (Song of Solomon 7.4).
>
> 'These shall not be eaten for they are an abomination: the eagle, the vulture, the buzzard, the kite . . . the hoopoe and the bat' (Leviticus 11.13–19).
>
> 'I permit no woman to teach or have authority over men; she is to keep silent' (1 Timothy 2.12).
>
> 'If your right eye causes you to sin, tear it out and throw it away' (Matthew 5.29).
>
> 'Love your enemies' (Matthew 5.44).

We certainly need all the help we can get in making sense of a book that presents us with such perplexities.

On Sunday we shall read the Bible in church as part of our worship. Here immediately are three principles about reading the Bible. *We* read the Bible. We read it *in church*. We read it *in worship*.

First, reading the Bible is something *we* do. It is good for me to read the Bible on my own, but it is bad for me to read the Bible only on my own. Being on one's own for too long with a Bible is as dangerous as being too long on one's own with a bottle or a gun.

Second, we read the Bible '*in church*'. That does not mean that we only read it when we're at a church service. It means that we read the Bible within the community of those who – however hesitantly and uncertainly – are seeking to walk the way of Jesus. It's a circle – scholars call it 'the hermeneutic circle'. What we believe about Jesus will be shaped by what the Bible says about him, but equally how we understand the Bible will be guided by what we have come to believe about Jesus. We read the Bible to get to know Jesus better, but as we get to know him better we read the Bible more perceptively.

We read the Bible 'in church'. There are, of course, other places to read the Bible. Many read the part of the Bible which we misleadingly call 'the Old Testament' in the synagogue. That is a good place to read the Bible. Christians should sometimes sit down with their Jewish sisters and brothers to read their scriptures together.

Third, we read the Bible in the context of *worship*. Again, that does not mean that I only read the Bible at Mass or Matins. It does mean that, whenever I read my Bible, I do so with the doors of my heart and mind and spirit open, prepared to be surprised by God.

The words of Jesus in the passage appointed as our Gospel are precisely located. The disciples have drawn Jesus's attention to 'the buildings of the temple' (Matthew 24.1). The immense stones, which formed the retaining walls of the platform on which the temple stood, are to this day a stupendous spectacle.

But the temple itself is gone, as Jesus said it would go. His prediction of its destruction is the prelude to all he goes on to say about what will precede 'the coming of the Son of Man'. Jesus's predictions pose huge problems. About the most difficult biblical texts to understand are those which talk about what will happen before all things come to an end.

Bible Sunday is not the day on which to try to read these runes. We pause instead on the words with which our Gospel concludes: 'Heaven and earth will pass away.' The temple is gone. But so too all our structures will go – all the things we build under the conceited illusion that they will last for ever, not least our own religious institutions. Whether all will end in a bang or a whimper, *all will end.* There will be no Bibles left, nor anyone left to read them.

Yet, says Jesus, 'My words will not pass away.' A simple and self-evident truth about the Bible is perhaps neither so simple nor so self-evident that it does not need repeating. Our Bibles will crumble into dust, just as will the hands that hold them. It is otherwise with the words of Jesus – and with the Word who is Jesus.

YEAR B

Isaiah 55.1–11; 2 Timothy 3.14—4.5; John 5.36–47

TRUE WITNESS

Fifty years ago I was urged to read a book with a title taken from our Gospel. *Search the Scriptures* is a three-year study guide to the Bible, first published in 1934. The book is still in print and widely used. It was written by the late Alan Stibbs, who was a fine scholar and a much-loved Christian teacher. Alan Stibbs believed, as do all conservative evangelical Christians, that the Bible is the Christian's supreme authority. It is the Bible that teaches us what to believe and how to live. Moreover, it does so *infallibly*. The Bible is the inspired Word of God and, because the Spirit of God cannot lie or mislead, it is inerrant.

How do we know that the Bible speaks truly and authoritatively? We know that the Bible is accurate and that it has the last word – so I was taught – because this was our Lord's view of Holy Scripture. Furthermore, it was what Paul believed. Words from our second reading were often drawn to our attention – 'All scripture is given by inspiration of God.' The circularity of the argument – we know that the Bible is inspired because 2 Timothy 3.16 says it is and we know that 2 Timothy 3.16 is inspired because it is in the Bible – did not trouble those who deployed it. The inerrancy of scripture was the premise they started from, not the conclusion they came to.

The exhortation 'Search the scriptures', which provides the title for Alan Stibbs's book, is taken from the Authorized Version's translation of the Bible. In fact it is a *mistranslation*. The Greek verb is an indicative, not an imperative, as all modern translations of the John 5.39 recognize. 'You search the scriptures,' says Jesus to his opponents, 'because you imagine that in them you have eternal life'. The Authorized Version allowed the text to be treated as a command to study the Bible zealously. In fact Jesus was saying that such a use of scripture is in itself futile.

According to John, Jesus boldly claims that these scriptures, our 'Old Testament', witness to him. Why is the Bible important? We do not beg any of the difficult questions about the Bible if we suggest that its unique importance lies in the *witness* it provides. The Bible testifies. It testifies to a people, to a person, and to a people.

The Hebrew scriptures testify to *a people*, a people whose story – as both Jews and Christians agree – is of the unfolding purpose of God for all humanity. The Gospel-writers testify to *a person*, to the mission and achievement of Jesus of Nazareth. In our own time the possibility is once again being canvassed that their witness is to be trusted. That is because, so it is once again claimed, the evangelists' record reflects faithfully eyewitness testimony. Behind the Gospels were those who could say, 'We declare to you what was from the beginning, what we have heard, what we have seen with our eyes, what we have looked at and touched with our hands concerning the word of life' (1 John 1.1).

The remaining books of the New Testament testify to *a people*. The Acts of the Apostles testifies to the emergence within Judaism of a people who looked to Jesus as the one in whom God's purpose for humanity is fulfilled. This people is simply the people of 'the way' (Acts 9.2). The rest of the New Testament witnesses to this people's attempt to articulate their faith in the one in whom, they believe, God has acted for the salvation of the world.

The scriptures testify. But testimony can take different forms. Testimony can be cool, detached and objective. Minutes, for example, are meant to be like that. They are supposed to be impartial. The more boring they are the better. Parliamentary debates can be impassioned; Hansard must never be. On the other hand, testimony can be intensely passionate, reflecting a commitment. An ardent lover's description of his beloved will be of that order. So will be the tribute of a son to the father he adored. The big bad mistake is to suppose that it is only testimony of the first sort – PCC minutes and the like – that speaks truly. But the witness that wells from the heart speaks truly too, just as truly as the neat notes of the PCC secretary or the Hansard clerk.

Scriptural testimony is of the second sort. It is the witness of the committed. That is why much of it is in poetry. That is why the prophet speaks truly when he promises the exiles in Babylon that, when their long captivity is over and they set off home, 'all the trees of the field shall clap their hands'. That is why the Bible is telling the truth in its witness to the resurrection of Jesus.

YEAR C

Isaiah 45.22–25; Romans 15.1–6; Luke 4.16–24

PROPHECY NOT PREDICTION

Matthew and Mark tell how Jesus, at some point in his ministry, came to his home town of Nazareth and taught in its synagogue. Both describe how those who heard him found his preaching offensive (Mark 6.15; Matthew 13.54–58). Luke, however, makes much more of this episode by placing it at the outset of his account of the mission of Jesus. For Luke, Jesus's sermon in the synagogue is the manifesto of his mission – and Jesus finds that manifesto in his Bible.

Jesus reads a text they will have known well, the prophet's vision of the messianic age, when poverty, physical affliction and oppression will be no more. The congregation would have heard the passage many times and, just as often, they would have listened to the same soothing sermon based on it, the consoling message that one day the prophet's dream would come true.

But the sermon they hear this time is not what they expect. Jesus does not say that one day the dream will come true, but that the dream comes true today! The scripture is fulfilled. He is the one, he tells them, who is anointed to inaugurate God's reign. The congregation's reaction to this extraordinary claim is astonishment and incredulity, swiftly followed by outrage and the first attempt on Jesus's life.

Scripture, says Jesus, is fulfilled – and fulfilled 'today'. A cluster of questions come to mind. In what sense is our Bible a prophetic book? If so, to what extent are its prophecies fulfilled and how far do they await fulfilment? And how can a text, written in such a remote 'yesterday', speak to our 'today'?

Prophecy has had a bad name. That is because we have confused it with prediction, the foretelling of what will happen in the far future. The confusion is rooted in the Bible itself. Some New Testament writers treat the Hebrew scriptures, our Old Testament, as a quarry in which, if you try hard enough, you can find verses predicting in detail events in the life of Jesus. To be sure, there were prophets who did predict, those to whom – so they claimed – God had revealed how the world would end. Often their predictions were couched in strange symbols that had to be decoded.

But prophecy and prediction are really quite different. The great prophets of the Bible, men like Isaiah or Jeremiah, Amos or Hosea, spoke to their contemporaries about their own time. If they talked of the future, it was not of the far future but of the near future, of what would ensue if their hearers did not mend their ways. Paradoxically, it is because the prophets spoke to *their* time that they speak so powerfully to *our* time. That is because the faith of the prophets is through and through ethical. What matters to them is not what might happen in the remote future, but how we should always live.

That is why the Bible is still a prophetic book. The prophets, who speak to their time, speak to all time, and so speak to our time. In the eighth century BC and in the twenty-first century AD, Micah utters the word of God,

> He has showed you, O man, what is good;
> and what does the LORD require of you
> but to do justice, and to love kindness,
> and to walk humbly with your God? (Micah 6.8)

Prophecy of this kind is not fulfilled by predicted events taking place. Micah's prophecy is fulfilled when it is *obeyed*. It is in this sense that Jesus is fulfilment of prophecy.

Whatever the circumstances of the nativity of Jesus, the text that Matthew took as predicting his virgin birth has nothing to do in its original context with such a birth centuries later (Isaiah 7.14; Matthew 1.23). Isaiah's reference was to an entirely normal birth about to take place. Jesus fulfils Old Testament prophecy, not by fulfilling predictions, but by perfectly embodying and obeying the pattern of redemptive suffering that the profoundest of the prophets saw written in the divine scheme of things (Isaiah 52.13—53.12).

The written 'word of God' is fulfilled by the obedience of Jesus Christ, the living Word of God.

> Although he was a Son, he learned obedience through what he suffered; and being made perfect he became the source of eternal salvation to all who obey him. (Hebrews 5.8–9)

Jesus fulfils scriptural prophecy by his obedience to its deepest truth. But the one who thus obeys prophecy is himself a prophet to be obeyed – or, to be scripturally accurate, he is 'the prophet' to be obeyed. The voice from the cloud on the Mount of Transfiguration says, 'This is my beloved Son. Hear him' (Mark 9.7). The words reflect the Greek text of Psalm 2.7. But they echo too what was said by Moses: 'The LORD your God will raise up for you a prophet like me ... Him you shall heed' (Deuteronomy 18.15).

Biblical prophecy is still to be fulfilled because we have yet to heed what Jesus says.

Mothering Sunday

Exodus 2.1–10 or 1 Samuel 1.20–28; 2 Corinthians 1.3–7 or Colossians 3.12–17; Luke 2.33–35 or John 19.25b–27

DAFFODILS AND TEARS

The Gospel-writers do not dwell on the harrowing details of the death of Jesus. Their reticence is not because the gruesome procedure of crucifixion was all too familiar to their first readers, nor is it to spare our squeamish feelings. The evangelists want us to understand who it is who suffers and why he suffers so, not to rehearse in every particular what he went through. The same restraint is used in describing those at the foot of the cross. We hear who are there but nothing of their pain. From Mary Magdalene 'seven demons had gone out' (Luke 8.2). What now possesses her mind we are not told.

The mother of Jesus is unnamed in John's Gospel. So too is the 'beloved disciple'. Those closest to the cross are the most hidden. We know that his mother's name is Mary, but the author of this Gospel purposely does not mention it. On Mothering Sunday we shall deplore the anonymity of motherhood, the fact that mothers have generally gone unmentioned in our histories, in the books with their telling titles, 'The History of Man' and the rest. We cannot accept that a mother's identity should be subsumed and lost in that of the man she has married or the son she has carried. But the anonymity of Mary in John's Gospel is not because she is overlooked. Later all generations will call her blessed. But had she spoken here at the cross, her word would have been the Baptist's: 'He must increase; I must decrease' (John 3.30).

The debate about the identity of 'the beloved disciple' will drag on until the day we meet him. Whoever he was, what mattered most to him was that he was loved by Jesus. For those who doubt whether anyone loves them, nothing can be more overwhelming than to find that they are wrong. The reason why one of Shakespeare's most cruel characters does some little good at the last is just because he makes this discovery. 'Yet Edmund was belov'd' (*King Lear* V. III. 239).

Jesus commends the unnamed woman and disciple to each other. At the foot of the cross a new community is formed. The death-throes of Jesus are the birth-pangs of the Church. It is the first meeting of the new family of God – all two of them, hiding together in the cleft rock.

A commentary on our cameo Gospel and on the relationship between Christ, his mother and the disciple he loved, are provided by a remarkable stained-glass window in Littlemore church, near Oxford. The church was built by John Henry Newman, though the window is later. The mother of Jesus and the beloved disciple are pictured at the foot of the cross. They are virtually embracing the cross, their figures almost merging with it, but at the same time – and very touchingly – they are holding hands. Bernard Schünemann, formerly Vicar of Littlemore, comments on this window, with its rare iconography: 'The agony and death of Jesus transforms our inability to form an intimate relationship with God.' His death puts us right with God. But what about each other? On Mothering Sunday, we wonder whether that agony and death can also transform our often wretched incompetence in relating to our nearest and dearest.

Newman's own difficulty was not an 'inability to form an intimate relationship with God'. He got on pretty well with God. Newman's problem was not God but mother. She disapproved of the direction her son's religious opinions were taking. 'I, who never thought of any thing more precious than her sympathy and praise,' wrote Newman, 'had none of it.' It is a pattern endlessly repeated. The child's guilt, carried over into adult life, that he or she can never be good enough; the parent's tormented sense of loss in watching their child go his or her own way. It is the most endemic of our disordered loves and by far the most destructive of our well-being. (The foundation stone of Littlemore church was laid by Newman's mother, though she did not live to see its consecration. Newman erected an absurd alabaster memorial to her, a monument showing her discussing the plans of the new church with an angel. Was Newman trying to assuage that crippling sense of guilt?)

On Mothering Sunday it is very important indeed that we give daffodils to Mums, but we trivialize this precious day if we evade its shadows. The adults we see weeping on Mothering Sunday are not all shedding tears of happiness.

O Lord Jesus Christ, fill me with that love of thine wherewith out of thine own pain thou didst comfort thy mother in hers; and, despoiled and naked, gavest her both home and son. To such love, without like, without limit, lead me, O Lord, now and for ever.
(Eric Milner-White, *A Procession of Passion Prayers*, SPCK, 1950)

Harvest Thanksgiving

YEAR A

Deuteronomy 8.7–18 or 28.1–14; 2 Corinthians 9.6–15; Luke 12.16–30 or 17.11–19

SURVIVAL AND SURFEIT

At Harvest we get down to earth, to the soil beneath our feet. In the earliest chapters of the Bible contrasting verdicts are pronounced on the earth. God sees that the earth is good – but he also says that it is cursed. 'God called the dry land Earth,' we read, '. . . and God saw that it was good' (Genesis 1.10). But turn a page and we have a different judgement passed on that same dry land. God says to the man he has made, 'Cursed is the ground because of you; in toil you shall eat of it all the days of your life . . . By the sweat of your face you shall eat bread' (Genesis 3.17–19).

The earth is good. The earth is cursed. Characteristically, the Bible holds both truths in tension. A dark thread running through the Bible's story is the experience of famine, of harvests that yield nothing but 'worthless heads of grain scorched by the east wind' (Genesis 41.27). The Bible repeatedly takes us into the desert, where the recalcitrance of the earth testifies to the primal curse on it. But equally the Bible witnesses, in language of unsurpassed loveliness, to the fruitfulness of the earth. So we sing,

The pastures of the wilderness overflow,
the hills gird themselves with joy,
the meadows clothe themselves with flocks,
the valleys deck themselves with grain,
they shout and sing together for joy. (Psalm 65.12–13)

At Harvest all we want to do is to celebrate. On such a day we do not want to hear about God's curse upon the earth. But fidelity to the Biblical account of the earth, as both blessed and blighted, means being less blinkered. So too, of course, does some slight awareness of the world beyond the church doors.

For most of our brothers and sisters – and not only in the so-called developing world – the cycle of planting and reaping, of seed-time and harvest, is an unremitting struggle for survival. According to the strange old story, it is Adam's doom that befalls us all. Certainly it befalls most of us. The tall tale of an outraged deity cursing the ground because of the folly of our first forefather, lately turned out of paradise, may be myth, but like every myth, it tells a truth about how things are. Most of the world's farmers are subsistence farmers. They thank God if they survive.

My friend Martin, who helped look after my garden when I lived in Africa, writes to me. 'You must have heard about the heavy rains in many regions which have brought a lot of damage to houses and crops. During this season we expected good crops, but as the rains increased crops and houses were destroyed, including mine near the riverside.' That was the little house he had built by himself, mud brick by mud brick.

The poor thank God if they survive. So too must those of us who have escaped poverty. Jesus teaches us to ask for our daily bread – for enough to get by, not for wealth for years to come – and we give thanks if that prayer is answered.

But what are we to do if we more than survive? Harvest challenges us to come to Christian terms with the experience of surfeit. Our choice of readings from Deuteronomy goes only so far in helping us meet this challenge. We may choose to hear Moses' warning: 'Take heed that you do not forget' (Deuteronomy 8.11). We take to heart the truth that there is nothing ours – even if it is more than enough – that is not given. Alternatively, we may choose to hear Moses' promise: 'Blessed shall be your basket and your kneading bowl' (Deuteronomy 28.5). Abundance and over-abundance will be ours – if, that is, we obey all that God commands. (On a busy Sunday, there will be no time to hear the rest of Deuteronomy 28, with its dire threats of the terrors that will overtake us if we don't do what God tells us. Nor will there be time to ask – with Job – whether in reality being pious always makes you prosperous.)

There is another passage from Deuteronomy which we should turn to, as well as – or instead of – the two we're supposed to choose from. The importance of this text is that it establishes the moral responsibility of those who are surfeited towards those who barely survive. Moses commands:

> When you reap your harvest in your field and forget a sheaf in the field, you shall not go back to get it; it shall be left for the alien, the orphan, and the widow, so that the LORD your God may bless you in all your undertakings. (Deuteronomy 24.19–22)

The same principle applies, Moses insists, in harvesting your olives and your grapes. It is not hard to guess what such a legislator would have had to say about third-world debt.

YEAR B

Joel 2.21–27; 1 Timothy 2.1–7 or 6.6–10; Matthew 6.25–33

GROUND LEVEL

Once I was a soldier in Berlin. On Sundays, when I wasn't soldiering, I ran a Sunday School. At Harvest Festival the Sunday School children would bring forward their gifts of vegetables and fruit and flowers to the front of the church. One year, General Rome, who commanded the garrison, agreed to stand at the front of the church to receive the gifts from the children. General Rome was a general and I was a corporal, and between generals and corporals a great gulf is fixed. So I was nervous, very anxious that the children would not let me down. Nor did they let me down. They all handed over their harvest gifts with great dignity and decorum – all except Vivienne, who was five. Vivienne was like God. She was no respecter of men. When her moment came, she skipped forward, thrust her bunch of flowers into the general's hands, and yelled at him – 'Now just you mind those. They're wet!'

Children puncture our self-importance and cut us down to size. Children are great levellers. So too is Harvest. At Harvest we are taught that, 'though we are many, we are one body, because we all share in one bread'. We say those words at Communion services. We are claiming that Christians, who gather round a communion table to receive bread and wine, share a common life. That is quite right. But it is not only Christians who are one body. The whole human race, the one human family, is one body.

What unites us is our need for bread. The 'bread' in different places may take different forms. It may be a plate of beans, or a bowl of borsch, or a Bombay duck. But it is still bread. Bread – that by which we are and without which we cease to be. All of us are united by our shared hunger and by the bread which satisfies it.

Shared hunger and shared bread abolish every distinction by which we divide and sub-divide our one humanity. The general needs his next meal as much as little Vivienne. Much good will all his medals and red tabs do him if he doesn't get it.

There is an unforgettable harvest story in Leo Tolstoy's great novel *Anna Karenina*. It describes how the rich landowner Levin joins in the annual haymaking on his vast estate. He goes out into the field where his peasants are working. These are his serfs, his personal property. Levin strips to the waist and takes a scythe. He steps into line between two of his peasants, and with them and in time with them, he begins to cut the hay. From dawn to dusk he works with them, harvesting the hay. To start with there is awkwardness on both sides and Levin is clumsy in his work. But as the hours pass Levin falls into the rhythm of those who have mowed hay every year since they were old enough to hold a scythe. And they no longer notice how strange it is that someone so exalted as their master Levin should be harvesting the hay with them. At the end of a row, Tolstoy tells us, an old man next to Levin stops to clean his scythe with a knot of grass. And then the old man takes his tin dipper, dips it into the stream, there at the edge of the field, and offers Levin a drink. And Tolstoy writes: 'Truly Levin had never tasted any drink so good as this warm water with bits of grass floating in it and with its rusty flavour from the tin dipper.'

That harvest was for Levin a levelling experience – as is every Christian celebration of harvest. At Harvest we recover our common humanity. All our absurd hierarchies, professional, ecclesiastical, military and all the others – all those pecking orders by which we set such store – cease to exist. We are, all of us, hungry people begging for bread.

The disciples of Jesus asked him to teach them how to pray. Jesus said, 'When you pray, say "Give us this day our daily bread".' Harvest sends us back to that primal prayer. We need to stress one word in that short bidding – 'Give *us* this day our daily bread.' Not 'give me' – but 'give us'. The 'us' is all-embracing. It is not only the 'us' who find their way to churches and eat holy bread from a holy table. It is the 'us' who survive by ordinary bread and the 'us' who, through lack of bread, fail to survive. Harvest brings us down to earth. It brings us down to the rich earth of the English countryside, but it also brings us down to the parched earth of our planet's dry places, to the dust bowls where the vulnerable starve. It brings us down to desiccated earth, where the Masai farmer hangs himself because all his cattle are dead.

YEAR C

Deuteronomy 26.1–11; Philippians 4.4–9 or Revelation 14.14–18; John 6.25–35

LOOK AFTER YOUR HOME

I vividly remember a Harvest Festival long ago. The church, set in cornfields, was approached by a bridle-path. It had been a glorious summer and now it was a golden autumn day. The church was overflowing with produce, with food and fruit and flowers grown in the fields and orchards and gardens of the parish. All the scents and sounds of the countryside flooded through the church's open doors. Many in that little house of God that Sunday still worked on the land. They were thanking God for what they themselves had 'safely gathered in'. (Though even that church was having to make peace with modernity. The previous week its ancient gas mantles had been removed and electric lighting installed.)

Such a celebration suited such a setting. Here were country people giving thanks for the fertility of the soil they themselves had worked, for the fecundity of the fields they themselves had harvested. There's rarely that kind of link between liturgy and life at Harvest Festivals these days, even in rural areas. Yet we go on singing the old harvest hymns, decking our churches as we have always done, nostalgic for a world that was never ours, wistful for a way of life we never knew. Even at St Martin-in-the-Fields, where I worked for a while, some aspects of our harvest celebrations gave the impression that the church was still surrounded by the fields that gave that famous church its name.

Is there still place for Harvest? There is. That is because we too belong to one community. We are as much one community as were country villagers a century ago. And we are just as dependent on the fruitfulness of the earth as they were, those who laboured all their lives on the fields around their parish church.

We have one small home – and it is in danger. Twenty years ago the United Nations convened a conference in Rio de Janeiro on sustainable development. Many of the agreements made at Rio have yet to be implemented. Subsequent attempts to secure and implement agreement among the nations about measures to sustain a habitable planet – at Kyoto and Copenhagen – have been more productive of rhetoric than of change. Nevertheless, since Rio we have recognized that we cannot for ever abuse the earth with impunity. All we have learned over the last two decades about how climate-change threatens the future of our life on earth only makes the warnings given at Rio the more urgent.

Even the Churches have woken up to the dangers we are in. There were many delegates from the Churches at the Rio conference. Afterwards they wrote 'A Letter to the Churches'. 'Dear sisters and brothers,' they began, 'we write with a sense of urgency. The earth is in peril. Our only home is in plain jeopardy. We are at the precipice of self-destruction. For the very first time in the history of creation, certain life-support systems of the planet are being destroyed by human actions.'

The apocalyptic tones of this letter are familiar to us from the New Testament, much of which was written in the fearful certainty that the time was short and that here we have no abiding city. The night is coming when no one can work. In our alternative second reading the imagery of harvest expresses how little time is left. The Son of Man is summoned. 'Use your sickle and reap,' he is exhorted, 'for the hour to reap has come, because the harvest of the earth is fully ripe.' The nervous editors of our lectionary call too swift a halt to the reading of this terrifying text. When we read on we hear of another with a sharp sickle, one who will gather the vintage of the earth and throw it into the great wine-press of the wrath of God. There it will be trodden 'outside the city' (Revelation 14.19–20). 'Outside the city' – where God in Christ, crucified 'outside the camp' (Hebrews 13.13), suffers to the end of time.

We are one small community, just as were those from the tiny village who came to church to give thanks for the crops they themselves had grown. To be sure, our home is a little bigger. Our fields extend beyond theirs. Our parish bounds are those of the round earth. The earth is the only home we have. It will not last for ever, any more than our bodies will. But just as we must not wilfully or neglectfully harm our flesh, so we must not maltreat our earth.

What must we do and where shall we go in what little time there may be left? Those who wrote from Rio said, 'The Spirit teaches us to go first to those places where community and creation are most obviously languishing, those melancholy places where the cry of the people and the cry of the earth are one.'